BUILT FROM THE QUIET

Secrets from a
Basque Sheepherder
that will Transform
Your Business and Life

Anamarie Lopategui

ISBN: 979-8-218-83016-8

For my Aita (father), Tiburcio Sarratea –

This book is for you, because of you, and in loving memory of all you taught me about life, business, and what truly matters.

Nire Aitarentzat, Tiburcio Sarratea –

Liburu hau zuretzat da, zuregatik da, eta maitasunez oroitzen dut bizitzari, negozioari eta benetan garrantzitsua denari buruz irakatsi zenidana.

TABLE OF CONTENTS

Prologue: The Choice That Changed Everything. 7

Chapter 1: The Roots That Run Deep 13

Chapter 2: Witches, Wisdom, and Mindset 21

Chapter 3: The Seeds of Entrepreneurship 31

Chapter 4: Just Keep Going: How Challenge Fuels
Persistence. 37

Chapter 5: Rise Up or Retreat: The Uncomfortable
Truth About Change 51

Chapter 6: The Courage to Create Your Own Path:
Innovation, Resourcefulness, and the Power of Failure . .69

Chapter 7: Adapt or Get Left Behind: The Role of
Curiosity in Business Evolution 83

Chapter 8: The Joy in Hard Work – Building Success
with Purpose. 99

Chapter 9: The Courage to Let Go: The Power of
Purpose, Permission, and Pride. 111

Chapter 10: Impact: The Wealth That Lasts. 129

Chapter 11: The Legacy We Build and Leave Behind . . .153

Epilogue: The Business of Becoming. 171

Acknowledgments 179

About the Author. 181

Life is shaped by the choices we make.
Every decision carves a path – the life we live,
the businesses we build, the dreams we chase,
and the legacies we leave behind.

Bizitza egiten ditugun aukeren arabera
moldatzen da. Erabakien bakoitzak bidea markatzen
du: bizi dugun bizitzak, eraikitzen ditugun
negozioek, atzetik ditugun ametsek eta atzean
uzten ditugun ondareek.

PROLOGUE

The Choice That Changed Everything

The night closed in, a blanket of darkness, as he scrambled up the jagged paths of the Pyrenees. The weight of his existence hung on his choices, heavier than the tattered sack on his back, a burden of hope and despair intertwined. He wasn't merely climbing; he was clawing against defeat, dodging armed patrols, and chasing survival, which seemed as distant as the cold, indifferent stars above.

His footing gave way on the edge of the rain-slicked path, and his heart seized as he began to slide. He stumbled forward, momentum dragging him into a wild tumble. Mud, rocks, and grass tore through his fingers as he grasped at anything to break his fall.

His back slammed against rocks and jutting roots as he rolled, his outstretched hand grasping at air before pitching over the edge of the slope.

When he finally came to a brutal and breathless halt, the wreckage of his desperation surrounded him. The sack, once filled with precious manzanilla tea leaves and goods meant to keep his family afloat, lay shredded and empty. Its contents were scattered to the wind, trampled by the livestock that had bolted in panic. He stared into the abyss below, broken and in pain. Survival no longer felt distant, it felt stolen.

He lay there for what felt like an eternity, his chest heaving, the cold seeping through his torn clothes and into his bones. Pain radiated through his body, sharp and unforgiving, but it was the weight of failure pressing down on him that threatened to crush him entirely. The boy's injuries told a grim story. He had fallen down the rugged mountain path – a place he knew as intimately as his own heartbeat from years of navigating its treacherous terrain. To falter there, in the very place he felt most capable, was a blow to both his body and his spirit.

His breath came in ragged bursts, each one a battle against the panic sealing off his throat. He could stay where he was, letting the dark consume him, clinging to the faint hope that someone might find him – or the more haunting possibility that no one ever would. Or he could force himself to get up and attempt the journey home unsure whether he could even make it, knowing it meant facing his parents' disappointment for returning battered and unable to finish the task they so desperately relied on him to complete.

Waiting meant surrender. So he pushed himself onto his elbows, the sharp sting of bruises and torn skin igniting stars in his vision. His fingers searched the ground around him, trembling as they closed around a sturdy branch half-buried in the mud. A walking stick, crude but steady. He hauled himself upright, leaning heavily on the stick as his legs shook beneath him. Each movement sent waves of pain through his body, but he gritted his teeth and pressed on.

The mountains were merciless, but the earth beneath his feet offered small mercies. A flat rock to rest against, another branch to steady his steps, a trickle of water from a nearby stream. He took each moment, each tiny blessing, as proof that he could do this – that he would do this.

His thoughts swirled, heavy with doubt and determination. Step by agonizing step, he moved forward. He wouldn't let this defeat him. The fall down the mountain might've taken his strength, blood, and even tears, but it wouldn't take his will.

As he moved painfully, slowly, through the darkness, one thing became achingly clear: This was a moment of choice. He could have waited, hoping someone would stumble across him, or resigned himself to the mountain's will. But instead, he chose to rise up, to fight, to press forward despite the pain and uncertainty. However, with every step, a different kind of agony gnawed at him – the fear of not being enough, of failing his family in ways that couldn't be undone. The choice to continue his arduous journey, born of desperation and willpower, wasn't just about survival; it was a battle against his own self-doubt, a reckoning with the weight of expectations. It was a declaration of his character. This became the foundation for facing every challenge that lay ahead.

*Growing up, my family's story was like
the roots of a tree – grounded, intertwined,
and deeply nourishing.*

*Hazten ari nintzela, nire familiaren istorioa
zuhaitz baten sustraien antzekoa zen: oinarri sendoa,
elkarri lotuta eta sakonki elikagarria.*

CHAPTER 1

The Roots That Run Deep

The Pyrenees Mountains are home to the Basque people, whose identity has long been known for an unwavering commitment to tradition, an incredible work ethic, and an unshakable sense of integrity. These values form the cornerstone of their culture, influencing everything from their daily lives to their enduring customs.

The Basque people, with their distinct language, culture, and traditions, are one of the oldest ethnic groups in Europe. Their origins trace back to the prehistoric peoples who lived in the mountainous regions of northern Spain and southern France, in the area known as the Basque Country. Dotted with picturesque villages, ancient trails, and lush pastures, these regions form a haven where nature and culture intertwine. Rich in biodiversity and steeped in history, their dramatic landscapes have inspired legends and remain a cherished part of Basque heritage; for the Basques this is home. For centuries, Basques have remained fiercely independent, preserving their unique identity despite being surrounded by larger and more powerful nations.

However, the Basque experience has also been marked by struggle. During the Spanish Civil War (1936-1939), the Basques faced unimaginable hardship. As the war raged on, their land became a battleground, and their people were divided between those who fought for the republic, and those who aligned with Francisco Franco's fascist regime. In 1937, the bombing of Gernika and many other Basque towns by Nazi planes, under the orders of Franco's forces, became a symbol of the destruction of Basque life and culture. It was a tragedy that scarred the people deeply, both emotionally and physically, and marked the beginning of a long and painful era of oppression.

Under Franco's dictatorship (1939-1975), the Basques were subjected to the harshest of measures to suppress their language, culture, and political rights. The use of the Basque language, Euskera, was banned in schools and public life, and Basque traditions were stripped away as the regime imposed a homogenous Spanish identity. For generations, the Basques lived in fear, their once-vibrant culture slowly suffocating under the weight of fascism.

During this dark period, many Basque families faced inconceivable choices. Economic hardship and a lack of opportunity within their homeland pushed some of them to make the heartbreaking decision to start over abroad, leaving behind family, friends, and the land that had been theirs for centuries. For some, the only hope of a better life lay in distant lands – America, Argentina, Mexico, and other countries, where they sought to rebuild their lives.

Leaving their homeland wasn't just about escaping poverty or seeking opportunity; it was about the deep-seated belief that a better future for themselves and their children could be found beyond the borders of their homeland. The pain of separating from loved ones, often not knowing when or if they would ever see each other again, was hard.

The decision to emigrate was not made lightly. For Basques, family is everything. Leaving family behind meant acknowledging that separation was a price they were willing to pay for a chance at freedom – freedom from oppression, fear, and the suffocating grip of Franco's regime.

The immigrant experience was far from easy. Many Basques arrived to foreign lands without knowing the language and without connections and resources. Yet, driven by the same determination that had fueled their ancestors for centuries, they built new lives, often working in laborious jobs, starting small businesses, and creating tight-knit communities to support one another. Through perseverance, they became the backbone of their new countries, although they never forgot the homeland they had left behind.

Echoes of the Basque Past, Footsteps of My Father

The mountains of the Baztan Valley didn't just shape the land, they shaped the boy who tumbled down their slopes – my father, Tiburcio Sarratea. The land was as fierce and unyielding as the people who called it home. For him, growing up meant surviving, and surviving meant shouldering responsibilities far beyond his years. By age 5, he was carrying hay up steep hillsides on his back, his tiny frame dwarfed by the load. When the hay packing was done, he was moving sheep from one grazing mountainside to another. By the age of 10, he was navigating the rugged Pyrenees, smuggling livestock and manzanilla tea leaves – treasured for their digestive benefits – in exchange for essentials or the money to buy them. He came from a family of 12 – two parents and 10 children; he was the fifth child among eight boys and two girls. His childhood was sacrificed to ensure his family's survival, trading play for responsibility. The stories he shared of those journeys made my own childhood feel indulgent by comparison.

When I look back on my childhood, I feel a profound sense of gratitude for the life I was given, even as a part of me longed for something different. While other kids spent their Saturdays kicking soccer balls in neatly mowed fields or running bases on dusty diamonds, I was learning the intricacies of an accordion, an instrument that seemed almost comically large for my small frame. While they gathered at parks or rode bikes down sunlit streets, I was busy helping my family care for a garden so vast it could only be described as a small farm.

Our backyard wasn't a place for play – it was a place of purpose. Rows of vegetables stretched toward the horizon, each planted with care and intention. Beyond the garden stood pens and coops, alive with the hum of sheep, rabbits, chickens, and steers. It was a world teeming with life and lessons, guided by my father's unwavering belief that everything should contribute, that nothing should exist without giving back.

My childhood wasn't about convenience; it was about connection. We planted seeds by the cycles of the moon, raised animals with care and respect, and treated the land as an equal partner in the rhythm of our lives. These traditions, passed down through generations, shaped me, grounding me in values of hard work, sustainability, and reverence for nature's cycles.

Growing up, my family's story was like the roots of a tree – grounded, intertwined, and deeply nourishing. As much as I loved the simplicity and joy of my childhood, there was always an underlying sense of duality. I felt grateful for my roots yet couldn't ignore the yearning to find my own place in a world that seemed so different from the one my parents had known.

Life is shaped by the choices we make. Every decision carves a path – the life we live, the businesses we build, the dreams we chase, and the legacies we leave behind. We don't always control the circumstances we find ourselves in, but we always have control over how we respond. The decisions we make create the bridge from where we are to where we really want to be. And the most significant choices – the ones that define who we are and what we leave behind – are rarely made in comfort.

Survival is not just about living;
it's about finding a way to rebuild, even if
the pieces never fit quite the same.

Biziraupena ez da bizitzea bakarrik;
berreraikitzeko modua aurkitzea da, piezak
inoiz berdin egokitu ez arren.

CHAPTER 2

Witches, Wisdom, and Mindset

Tiburcio stumbled through the door of his home, wheezing, battered, bruised, and barely standing. My father, though just a boy then, carried more than the sharp pain searing through his body – he bore the weight of something far heavier. The crushing sense of failure. The disappointment was a wound all its own, one that pierced deeper than any broken bone.

My grandmother, pale with worry, wasted no time summoning the town doctor, her hands trembling as she clung to hope that her son could be saved. The doctor arrived, his face grim as he assessed the damage. Broken bones, internal injuries, and an uncertain prognosis painted a bleak picture. He worked methodically, doing everything within his power to mend what was broken. But as he wrapped splints and murmured reassurances, the unspoken truth hung heavy in the room: The internal injuries were a question mark, a fragile unknown that no amount of skill or care could address.

For my father, Tiburcio, the weight of uncertainty stretched beyond his battered body. It wasn't just the question of whether he would heal, it was the question of what came next. At only 16 years old, he was too young to understand his own mortality, but he was old enough to understand his current life. How could he return to the life he'd known, the life that demanded strength, courage, and purpose – a purpose that he no longer felt? The traditions of his upbringing closed in on him, intensifying his own expectations and amplifying the fear that he might not be able to meet them. The need to prove his worth gripped him.

And yet, even in this moment of crushing doubt and despair, a flicker of something remained. It wasn't hope – not yet. It was something rawer, more unyielding: a stubborn resolve buried deep beneath the weight of pain and the unknown.

The doctor's words pierced the silence like a blade. He told the family that the next few days would reveal whether Tiburcio would survive and it would be months before they'd know whether he could truly heal. He left them with the final thought that even if the boy did heal, it's doubtful he would ever return to the life he'd known. The words landed heavily, an unspoken challenge as much as a diagnosis. My grandmother grasped at hope despite the somber tone, while my father absorbed the weight of what was said – and what was left unsaid. Survival wasn't just about living; it was about finding a way to rebuild, even if the pieces would never fit quite the same.

By the grace of God, the tireless care of his family, and perhaps something beyond human comprehension, my father survived the night. Against the odds, his body clung to life. But it was clear from the start, survival was just the beginning.

The months that followed were hard. Bones slowly fused themselves back together, but the deeper, unseen wounds were slower to heal. Every breath was an effort, shallow and strained, as though the air itself carried the weight of his brokenness. His once-strong frame had withered, muscles wasting away due to immobility. The vibrant boy who had once roamed the rugged mountains with unyielding confidence now felt trapped in a body that no longer served him.

Would he ever reclaim what was lost? Could his body, once a source of strength and pride, ever become his own again?

My grandmother, embodying the resilience and wisdom of Basque women, turned to a path less traveled. The family managed to scrape together the resources, and she made the decision to take him to a *sorgina* (plural: *sorginak*) – a figure often referred to as a "witch" in English. The *sorginak* have often been misunderstood and misrepresented throughout history.

In Basque culture, the word *sorgina* is derived from *sor*, meaning to create, and *gine*, meaning female or woman, reflecting their role as creators, healers, and wise women deeply connected to the natural world. These women were often midwives, herbalists, or spiritual guides, revered for their knowledge of the earth's healing properties and their ability to nurture life. However, as in many other cultures, historical events distorted their image, turning them into "witches" during periods of religious and social upheaval.

In the early 17th century, a wave of witch hunts swept through Europe, fueled by fear, superstition, and the Spanish Inquisition's efforts to root out perceived heresy. Not far from my father's village, straddling the French-Spanish border, a small town named Zugarramurdi became infamous during those years, due to its strong traditions of the *sorginak* and those who came after them.

The Zugarramurdi caves were places of gathering, celebration, and ritual, where locals – especially women – would come together to honor the cycles of nature, share knowledge, and foster community bonds. These gatherings were seen as threatening by the Inquisition, which equated them with diabolical practices or witchcraft. What followed was a tragic series of interrogations, trials, and punishments. Ultimately these witch trials led to the burning of 11 people at the stake, while others were imprisoned or forced to confess under torture. Most of those accused were innocent, victims of social or religious rivalries or simply misunderstood for their cultural practices. This period left a dark mark on Basque history, although it also highlighted the community's deep ties to its traditions.

The *sorginak*'s practices were deeply rooted in ancient Basque healing traditions, predating Western medicine, Catholicism, and much of what is commonly recognized today. They were not "witches" in the malevolent sense imposed by the Inquisition. They were caretakers of knowledge about healing herbs, natural remedies, and ancient rituals tied to the cycles of the land, which offered support during illness and times of crisis.

I often wonder if my grandmother's wisdom stemmed from the deep-rooted knowledge of that region – a place where ancient traditions and a profound connection to the earth endured. Perhaps it was this shared cultural inheritance – a quiet understanding passed down through generations – that guided her to turn to a *sorgina* when modern medicine could offer no further healing or hope for her young son. Seeking out a *sorgina* was not a rejection of medicine or faith, but her best effort, trusting in the timeless wisdom that had sustained her people for centuries.

For six months, my father underwent treatments that combined the *sorginak*'s ancestral wisdom with his own resolve to heal. It wasn't just his body that mended; his spirit found strength in the process. Healing wasn't merely about his physical recovery; it became an act of willpower, a reclamation of his life and identity.

At 16 years old, broken but filled with hope, my father found solace in the care of the *sorgina*, who gently nurtured both his body and spirit back to health. The aftermath of a near-fatal fall had forced him to confront the brutal reality of his life. On that dark night, when he hung between life and death, a single question pierced through the haze of his pain: Should he give in to the darkness or fight for a better life?

The choice, though excruciating, was clear. Survival wasn't just about living another day, it was about making the most of each day – it was about purpose. While slowly regaining strength, he allowed hope to seep into the cracks of his despair. The whispers about America that he had heard long before his fall – a land of possibility, opportunity, and hope – became a lifeline. They painted a vision of a future he couldn't yet grasp but knew he had to pursue. First, he needed to heal. Then, he had to plan carefully. Years later, that vision began to take shape, transforming into reality.

In 1963, with a bag too small to hold all his hopes, he left all he knew behind to come to the United States to herd sheep in the Sierra Nevada Mountains of Nevada and California. He spoke no English and had no safety net or guarantees – just hope and an iron will. The loneliness of those mountains is something I can hardly fathom – weeks on end with only sheep and family memories for company. While by this time three of his siblings had already flown the nest, with two brothers moving to America and one sister to France, he was living alone. Even in isolation, he never lost sight of the life he was determined to build.

Tiburcio spent five years as a sheepherder, trading that time and labor for passage to America along with a small wage and monthly food allotment. When his contract ended, he headed to town and got his first paying job away from the loneliness of the mountains. Instead of tending thousands of sheep, he became responsible for milking hundreds of cows at a dairy in Genoa, Nevada.

His days were spent ensuring that the dairy ran smoothly, while weekends became a time for connection and exploration. With five of his brothers also now settling nearby, he forged a new community of family and friends. Together, they frequented Basque restaurants, fished in the mountains, and explored the open roads of their new home country.

Little did he know, one of those evenings socializing at a Basque restaurant would lead him to meet my mother.

My parents' love story began at a dance at the JT Basque Boarding House and Restaurant in Gardnerville, Nevada – a meeting that would intertwine two deeply rooted Basque souls. Both proudly 100% Basque, their shared heritage became the foundation of their lifelong bond.

Business, much like my father's journey, is rarely a straight path. There are falls – some so brutal they make you question everything. The weight of failure, pressure, and expectations can feel unbearable. But just like he did, we must choose: Do we give in to the setbacks or do we find a way to rebuild? The journey of an entrepreneur, like that of a survivor, is one of resilience, reinvention, and an unshakable belief that something better lies ahead. It starts with finding the strength to rise up, adapt, and push forward even when the odds are against us.

The journey of an entrepreneur, like that of a survivor, is one of resilience, reinvention, and an unshakable belief that something better lies ahead.

Ekintzaile baten bidaia, bizirik iraun duen batena bezala, erresilientzia, berrasmatze eta aurretik zerbait hobea dagoelako sinesmen irmoa da.

CHAPTER 3

The Seeds of Entrepreneurship

The roots of my entrepreneurial journey were planted long before I understood what entrepreneurship even was. One of the earliest sparks took hold in the backyard of my Aitatxi's house - my Grandpa Beñat, as we called him in Euskara, the Basque language - where curiosity, creativity, and a love for building things began to grow. I spent countless sun-soaked afternoons playing with my cousins. It wasn't a typical playground; it was a canvas for our imaginations and, in hindsight, the birthplace of my business drive. But the foundation for all of this was laid by something much deeper – the stories of my parents and grandparents, their incredible work ethic, and the heritage they carried with them from the Basque Country.

My mother's path as a first-generation American was different from my father's in many ways, yet equally infused with the unyielding Basque spirit. She was shaped by the sacrifices of my grandparents, who, like so many immigrants, came to the United States in search of a better life. Like my father, my grandfather was a sheepherder for nearly 17 years. He worked tirelessly to build a future for his family. His life wasn't easy, but it was driven by hope for the next generation – a hope that passed down to my mother and then to me.

My father's grit, courage, and zest for life perfectly complemented my mother's quiet strength, unwavering support, and warmth. Together, they built a life that honored our Basque heritage while navigating the challenges of raising a family and striving for the promise of the American Dream. Their love was more than a partnership – rooted in perseverance, it stood as a testament to resilience, hard work, and shared dreams.

Those roots found their way into every nook of my childhood, even Grandpa Beñat's house. His home was more than just a house; it was the place of so many childhood memories. While my parents were busy working, my sister and I along with our many cousins would spend our days there. It was a place where the richness of Basque culture came alive in the smells of the kitchen, the laughter of cousins, and the games we created with our imaginations and the simple things we could find in the house and yard. My grandfather's house was where tradition met the chaos of childhood, where the past flowed effortlessly into the present. It was, much like my father's story, a bridge. It connected the sacrifices of one generation to the dreams of the next, grounding us in who we were while giving us the freedom to explore who we could become.

That backyard wasn't just a place for play – it was a land of possibility. We created every type of business we needed to make our little backyard a complete and thriving community. We had a bank, a school, a casino (born and raised Nevadan, after all), a hair salon, a restaurant, and even a taxi service, complete with an old, rusty wheelbarrow as our vehicle. My cousins and I dove headfirst into this imaginary community, each of us owning and operating our own "business."

I always owned and ran the restaurant – serendipitously, I ended up owning a real restaurant later. My excitement was endless as I created menus, posted daily specials on the chalkboard, organized the "kitchen," and proudly served customers. We didn't just stop at running individual businesses; we collaborated to make our backyard economy work. Marbles were the core of every casino game, the salon was always in the covered patio area using the best outdoor chair, and the restaurant was the small playhouse my grandfather built many years before - it housed the kitchen. I coordinated rides with the "taxi driver," whose wheelbarrow service often tipped over the "customers" before they reached their destination. Somehow, we always found a way to make it work – with plenty of laughter along the way.

As I close my eyes and think back to those sunny afternoons in Grandpa Beñat's backyard, I'm struck by how much those early days of play shaped my perspective on business and life. What started as simple, inventive games became the foundation of a lifelong love for entrepreneurship. Those chaotic yet organized "business ventures" taught me the value of creativity, problem-solving, and resourcefulness – and, most importantly, the sheer joy of building something from nothing.

Looking back now, I'm amazed at how those moments mirrored the real-world lessons of business. There was no problem too big, no challenge too overwhelming. If we needed a solution, we found one, even if it meant sneaking resources that were technically off-limits. It was in that backyard that I first discovered the power of curiosity, teamwork, adaptability, and creativity – the very traits that would later guide me through the real-world challenges of running a business.

The universe works in mysterious ways. That little girl playing restaurant wasn't just engaging in make-believe; she was unknowingly manifesting her future.

Persistence isn't just about determination, it's also the unwavering belief that effort, resilience, and sheer will can outlast even the hardest seasons.

Iraunkortasuna ez da determinazioa bakarrik, ahaleginak, erresilientziak eta borondate hutsak denboraldi gogorrenak ere gainditu ditzaketela dioen sinesmen irmoa ere bada.

CHAPTER 4

Just Keep Going: How Challenge Fuels Persistence

My father, the boy who survived a horrific fall down a mountainside, carried the scars of that moment not as a burden, but as proof of the human spirit's ability to endure. That fall wasn't just an accident – it was a lesson in survival, in picking yourself up when the ground beneath you crumbles. And in many ways, it foreshadowed the life he would go on to live. When he made his way to America, he didn't just carry the hope of a better future; he carried the unwavering belief that even the harshest circumstances could be transformed into opportunity. His survival wasn't just a moment of triumph – it became the foundation of an unrelenting drive to keep moving forward, no matter how impossible the road ahead seemed.

Like many Basques of his time, my father immigrated to the United States to work as a sheepherder. It was one of the few opportunities available to Basques, as sheepmen of the American West actively sought them out for their steadfast work ethic, reliability, and integrity – qualities proven by the generations who came before them.

Sheep provided multiple revenue streams, including wool and meat (lamb and mutton) for the ranchers of the American West. Wool was a highly valuable commodity, especially during wartime and in colder climates, making sheep ranching a profitable business. Sheep could graze on lands that were often unsuitable for cattle. They thrived in arid, rugged terrain and could eat a variety of plants, including weeds and brush, making them valuable for land management.

Sheepherding wasn't a calling for my father. It wasn't a dream or a passion. It was a means to an end, a stepping stone to something greater. He knew that if he committed, endured, and fulfilled his contract, it might open doors he had never even dared to imagine. But that didn't make it any easier.

For a man as social as my father, sheepherding in his 20s wasn't just hard, it was isolating. The days were long, the nights even longer. He lived in an endless cycle of blistering heat and bitter cold, making do with the most meager of supplies, cooking meals over an open flame with whatever he had on hand. He carried every possession he owned with him, packing and unpacking his life over and over again, following the rhythm of the flock. And always, he was relentlessly on the lookout – watching for coyotes lurking in the shadows, for predators waiting for a moment of weakness, for dangers that could wipe out everything he was responsible for in an instant.

But the greatest danger wasn't what lurked in the wilderness. It was the silence.

Like so many Basque sheepherders of his time, my father spent his most formative years utterly alone, lost in landscapes that stretched endlessly in every direction, with nothing but his thoughts to keep him company. The years that shape our desires, our ambitions, our understanding of the world – he spent those years in solitude. No conversations, no laughter, no one to share the weight of the days with. Just an expanse of land, the bleating of sheep, and the constant hum of longing for something more.

Ranchers relied on seasonal grazing, moving sheep between lower pastures in winter and mountain ranges in summer to ensure fresh forage. Sheepherders like my father were essential in managing these remote herds, walking many hundreds of miles over rugged terrain to guide the sheep from one grazing area to another.

If the grazing was thick and rich, they could linger in a spot for a few days, but their job was never idle.

A sheepherder's primary responsibility was to keep the flock moving in the right direction, ensuring that the sheep didn't overgraze or stray too far. Maintaining this delicate balance was crucial, not only for the health of the herd but also for the land itself. Overgrazing could strip the landscape, while careful movement allowed the plants and soil to recover.

Each day was part of an endless journey filled with many miles on foot, navigating valleys and mountain ranges under the vast Western sky.

It wasn't just hard work. It was a silent sacrifice.

But he kept going.

Because as much as the loneliness tried to break him, as much as the mountains and valleys swallowed his days, he knew this was temporary. This was the price he had to pay. He endured not because he loved the work, but because he refused to accept that this was all there was. He turned the hardship into a game – pushing himself to herd more sheep, to minimize losses, to raise the healthiest lambs, to make each year better than the last. Every penny he saved, every challenge he overcame, got him one step closer to something more. A driver's license. A car. A road to freedom. A future beyond survival.

And so he pushed on. Day after day. Month after month. Year after year.

Persistence isn't just about determination, it's also the unwavering belief that effort, resilience, and sheer will can outlast even the hardest seasons. My father didn't just teach me this. He lived it. His story wasn't just one of survival – it was a masterclass in refusing to accept anything less than the life he dreamed of.

Growing up, I didn't fully grasp the power of persistence, but I felt it. It seeped into my bones, becoming my mantra long before I understood the word. Perhaps it was woven into my DNA, passed down like a gift from my father. Watching him, I learned that persistence wasn't just about enduring; it was about believing that if you just kept going, no matter the challenge, you would succeed in what you set out to do.

At 13, I channeled my persistence into something I craved: soccer.

For years, I begged my parents to let me join an organized sports team. I wanted it so badly – not just to play, but to be part of what the other kids at school talked about, to experience the thrill of competition, to finally fit in. I understood competition well; we created it in everything we did: chores, backyard games, even the way we tackled responsibilities. But organized sports? That was different. It was a battle where everyone was chasing the same goal – literally. And I wanted in.

My pleading wasn't a passing request – it was insistent. Tears, promises, and constant persuasion became part of my daily routine until, finally, they gave in.

Stepping onto that field for the first time wasn't just about playing a sport; it was a victory born of sheer determination. I wasn't the most skilled player, but I was a hard worker. Every practice, every game, I heard my father's voice: *Just keep working.*

But for me, belonging on the team was never enough. I didn't just want to play; I wanted to excel. Every missed opportunity, every misstep, every time I was beaten by an offender was a lesson to do better next time. I wasn't afraid to fall short because each stumble taught me how to get back up. Persistence became my silent partner, pushing me to find solutions, improve my skills, and keep going.

The following fall, my persistence faced its next challenge: joining the boys' high school soccer team. There was no girls' team, and all the girls I played with the previous fall in league soccer decided to play volleyball, the recognized girl's option for high school team sports. I didn't want to learn how to play volleyball. For one thing, I was barely approaching five feet tall – not the typical stature for a volleyball player. Also, I had just begun to understand the game of soccer and finally started developing some skill, and I wanted to keep going. So I made the hard decision to try out for the boys' team.

I wasn't the only girl trying out. A few older girls were there too and, on that first day, I watched them play – confident, fearless, competing with the boys. Watching them, something clicked. If they could do it, so could I.

But after that first day, reality hit hard. If I wanted to make the team – and actually play – I had to get better. Fast. I needed to be stronger, to compete physically, without getting pushed off the ball. The thought of sitting on the sidelines was unbearable. I was wildly underprepared – after all, I'd been playing for less than a year – but I refused to let that stop me.

For the next three days, I gave everything I had. Then came the wait.

The roster would be posted at the field, taped to a fence post. That list would determine everything. I had never felt the weight of anticipation like I did that day, equal parts excitement and dread. What if my name wasn't there?

Finally, I hitched a ride with my sister and made my way to the field. My heart pounded as I scanned the list, searching for my name. And then – there it was!

I had earned my spot. And I wasn't going to waste it.

From day one, I trained harder than I thought possible, knowing I had to prove myself every single day. I wasn't as skilled or experienced as my teammates.

In practice, I got beat, constantly, and barely saw game time unless we were ahead. But I refused to back down. I kept showing up. I kept pushing. I kept getting better.

By the end of the season, I had finally earned my place – not as the token girl, but as a player who belonged.

That year taught me something invaluable: Growth demands stepping into spaces that stretch you. It means surrounding yourself with people who are bigger, faster, and better than you – and using that discomfort to develop and flourish.

Growth isn't comfortable. But it was worth it.

Over the next three years, girls' high school soccer became an officially recognized sport, and I kept playing. By my senior year, I knew one thing for sure – I wanted to keep playing beyond high school.

The problem? I had no idea how.

My parents weren't familiar with the college process, let alone what it took to play sports at the next level. What I quickly realized was that I was already late to the game. Most players had been scouted, recruited, or had connections guiding them through the process. I had none of that.

Still, I refused to give up. I started searching for any opportunity to play, eventually reaching out to the coach at UC-Davis, a school not far from my hometown.

I sent my stats, awards – anything that might get me a chance.

The response? A yes.

If I could get accepted academically, I'd be invited to preseason training and given a shot at tryouts.

It wasn't a guarantee. It wasn't a scholarship. But it was a chance.

And that was enough to give me hope. And in the end, that was all that was needed. I was accepted and began my freshman year at UC-Davis.

On the first day of preseason, I was completely intimidated. The other players swapped stories about the ultra-competitive clubs they had played for and their years of experience. I didn't have that kind of background, and I felt like I was trying to compete in a world where I didn't belong. For the first time in three years, I was stuck in my own head. My biggest roadblock wasn't my skill or ability – it was me.

When official tryouts arrived, I was just another hopeful among many, fighting for a spot. Had I played with confidence, had I let myself just enjoy the game I loved, my preseason invitation might have worked in my favor. I could have made an impression, shown what I was truly capable of. But I didn't. Instead, tryouts felt just like preseason – like I wasn't even in control of my own body. The player on that field was intimidated, timid, scared, and weak. I played small. I shrank into the background. And I didn't make the team.

I was crushed. But I knew exactly why.

I hadn't shown up as the player who wanted to compete. I had shown up as the player who was already defeated.

So, there I was at an expensive, highly competitive academic school where I struggled both academically and financially. Calculus 101. Chemistry 101. Hundreds of students packed into lecture halls. I felt lost in a sea of academically driven students who all seemed so much smarter than me.

Meanwhile, I was juggling three jobs, painfully aware of the heavy tuition and living expenses my family could barely afford. And worst of all? I missed playing soccer.

I still didn't know what I wanted to be when I grew up, but I knew one thing for certain: I loved the focus, fire, and purpose that competitive sports had given me. And now, that part of me was missing.

By the second half of the year, I knew I had to try again. I wasn't ready to let go of my dream.

So I started researching every competitive community college soccer program in California. I reached out to coaches, hunted for opportunities to play during the spring and summer – anything to get back on the field. After many phone calls and drives to neighboring California junior colleges, I found the place that felt right. I went to as many preseason spring trainings that my school and work schedule would allow with a completely different mindset: I had nothing to lose.

Late that summer, I tried out for the Santa Rosa Junior College's team – and I made it. Not only did I make it, but I was also given a tuition reduction in exchange for being on the starting roster. With an incredible coach, a talented group of teammates, and sheer determination, I thrived. I went from barely maintaining a 2.0 GPA to becoming a 4.0 student, excelling in my beloved science courses. My tuition and rent for two years amounted to pennies in comparison to my first year of college, and for the first time in a long time, I felt like I was exactly where I was meant to be.

By the end of those two years, I knew I wanted to finish my college career playing soccer and getting my education paid for. With the help of my coach, I secured an offer to transfer and continue playing for a Division 1 school. As our season came to a close, we reached the semifinals for the regional title. This was my last chance to leave it all on the field, playing for the coach who had given me so much.

With five minutes left in the game, we were up 1-0. As I charged toward the ball, challenging an opposing player, my leg gave way. A sharp, excruciating pain shot through me, followed by the unmistakable sound of a pop. I tried to get up, but something was wrong. I couldn't move. I couldn't run. This pop would ultimately change my path, change my degree, and point me in the direction of a career that wasn't in the plan.

Sheepherding, soccer, and business may seem like entirely different worlds, but the lesson is the same: Success isn't about avoiding challenges, it's about deciding to keep going despite them. On the field, I learned that you don't rise up by playing it safe – you rise up by stepping into discomfort, by competing against those who are stronger, faster, and more experienced. In sheepherding, my father knew that success depended on patience, problem-solving, and the ability to adjust when things didn't go as planned. Sheep don't always move the way you want them to. Sometimes they scatter. Sometimes they refuse to budge. And sometimes, lurking in the night, is a coyote waiting to strike – forcing you to think fast, pivot, and protect what's yours.

Business is no different. Your plan won't always unfold the way you expect. The market shifts, competitors move in, employees move on, and unforeseen obstacles arise. In both cases, the real work isn't in the moments when everything is running smoothly, it's in the moments when everything feels impossible. The missed shot, the failed tryout, the injury. The slow sales month, the unexpected expense, the idea that didn't land. Those moments don't just test your skill, they test your resolve. They force you to ask yourself: How bad do you want this? Will you let the setback define you, or will you find a way forward?

In business, persistence is what separates those who succeed from those who don't. It's not just talent, strategy, or even luck. It's about pushing through setbacks, adapting when things don't go as planned, and showing up even when it's hard. Challenges aren't roadblocks; they're part of the process. Success isn't built in a single win, a single sale, or a single breakthrough. It's built in the choice you make every day – to keep going, figuring it out and refusing to quit. So the question is: When things get hard, will you back down or will you persist, adapt, and keep moving forward?

Success isn't about avoiding challenges,
it's about deciding to keep going despite them.

Arrakasta ez da erronkak saihestea, baizik eta
haien aurrean ere aurrera jarraitzea erabakitzea.

CHAPTER 5

Rise Up or Retreat:
The Uncomfortable Truth
About Change

For many Basque immigrant sheepherders, the path to America was built on contracts and promises, often fragile and sometimes broken. These men arrived with little more than a signed contract, a passport, and a heart full of hope. The deal was simple: If you worked hard and fulfilled your contract, in return you'd get legal residency – a green card, your golden ticket to a better life.

Sheep outfits, the companies that hired sheepherders, were supposed to handle the paperwork to apply for the green cards once the contracts were close to completion or fulfilled. That was the promise. But like most things tied to survival and power, it wasn't always that simple.

Technically, the green cards belonged to the sheepherders. But in reality? They were often held by the bosses. On the surface, it made sense. Life in the remote, unforgiving mountains was tough, and losing such an important document out there would be a nightmare. For almost all sheep bosses, it was genuinely about keeping the card safe. But for my father's? It was about control.

Without that green card in hand, he couldn't fully step into the freedom he had earned. It was a quiet kind of leverage – subtle but powerful. A way to keep him tied to work he no longer had to do, bound by the very promise that was supposed to set him free.

Years later, my father shared one of the most profound lessons from his time as a sheepherder – a job he took out of necessity, not passion. After all it was his path to America and chance at a better life.

He had signed a three-year contract to herd sheep in exchange for legal residency. When his contract ended, he agreed to stay a few extra months until a replacement was found – not because he loved the work, but out of respect and a sense of responsibility. Yet months turned into years, and still, no one came. He had fulfilled his end of the deal, but his green card remained out of reach, always met with excuses: *It's safer if we keep it. You don't want to lose it in the mountains.*

Still, he persisted. Every time he saw his boss, he asked for his green card. Again and again, he refused to back down. He was relentless.

Eventually, patience gave way to resolve. No more waiting. No more excuses. He laid it out plainly – either he would be given the green card or he would walk, leaving the boss to handle the work himself until a replacement could be found.

The ultimatum worked. His boss finally understood – this wasn't a bluff. Losing him wasn't just inconvenient; it would be a disaster. And the thought of doing the job himself? Unthinkable.

So, at last, my father secured his green card – the first real step toward the freedom he had envisioned.

And yet, even with his golden ticket in hand, he stayed. True to his word, he waited for the replacement that never came.

As he navigated the rugged expanse between Dayton, Nevada, and the unforgiving peaks of the Sierra Nevadas, he endured harsh conditions, bitter isolation, and the indifference of a boss who cared little for the well-being of his workers or the sheep they were tasked to protect.

For most Basque sheepherders, the experience, though grueling, was marked by mutual respect. Their bosses valued their expertise, listened when real problems arose, and ensured they had the necessary supplies, food, and support to endure the isolation of the mountains. Many sheep bosses had once been sheepherders and they not only understood what the job entailed, they lived the life. They were leaders who had walked in the same shoes and had deep respect for those who followed in their footsteps. But my father's story was different, and he didn't talk about it for many years. His boss was indifferent at best, dismissive at worst, and the hardships he faced were not just part of the job – they were unnecessary struggles imposed by someone who simply didn't care. Food deliveries were sporadic and unreliable, often containing just enough to get by… if you stretched it carefully. But even stretching supplies couldn't make up for food that arrived moldy, rancid, or spoiled.

After nearly two extra years beyond his contract, he began to question whether they had ever intended to find his replacement. But those years gave him something more than hardship. They instilled in him a steadfast persistence and planted a seed. A deep, growing motivation for independence and freedom that would shape the rest of his life.

The breaking point came when he was once again sent to manage thousands of sheep in a barren, unforgiving area where nutritious feed was scarce and toxic plants thrived. He had been there before – forced to stand by, helpless, as the sheep grazed out of desperation, consuming poisonous plants that wreaked havoc on their bodies. He watched them grow sick, trembling with weakness, and suffering in silent agony. His warnings to the boss fell on deaf ears again. The suffering of the sheep didn't matter and neither did his own. Days passed without proper supplies, leaving both him and the animals in desperate conditions.

My father's resolve hardened with every passing moment. He could no longer stomach watching the animals entrusted to his care suffer unnecessarily, nor could he endure the utter disregard for human dignity shown by those in charge. One day, in the perpetual quiet of the mountains, he made a decision that would define the rest of his life.

With hands weathered by years of hard work, he burned his canvas tent – his only shelter – along with almost every belonging he had. The flames reached into the sky, a symbol of defiance against the life he refused to endure any longer. It wasn't just an act of rebellion; it was a declaration of independence, a fiery proclamation that he would no longer allow others to dictate his future.

That day, with just a few possessions in his pockets, his small bag that traveled to America with him, and the clothes on his back, he hitched a ride to town with a passing rancher, leaving behind the mountains, the sheep, and the life that had stripped him of dignity. He told the rancher to pass along one simple message to his boss: *I'm done.*

That moment marked the beginning of something new. It was more than an escape – it was a choice. A choice to reclaim his dream, to create a life where his values, not someone else's indifference, defined his path. From that day forward, my father began building a life on his own terms, one step at a time, with a persistence and resolve forged in the fires of hardship. His final acts of defiance as a sheepherder – burning that tent and walking away – represented his determination to pursue new opportunities.

A few days later, he found himself in Carson Valley in the quiet little town of Genoa, Nevada. He took a job as a dairyman, milking hundreds of cows twice a day. The pay was better than sheepherding, and the job came with a small house at the dairy, making his commute almost nonexistent. Life was still hard, but he was freer.

Days were long – early mornings, regimented schedules, a long list of tasks between milkings. But on weekends, between milkings and after the second milking, he'd jump into his blue Malibu sports car, a prized possession bought with the money he'd saved from herding sheep. With his five brothers – who had also all made their way to America by his side – he'd drive through Gardnerville, Carson City, Reno, and take the winding roads to Lake Tahoe. Some weekends, instead of cruising the streets, they'd go fishing, finding peace in the mountains, in nature, in brotherhood.

For him, this was freedom. Life was simple, but full.

During his years at the dairy, he met my mother. They fell in love and the wedding was a celebrated affair, uniting two Basque families coming together as one, to honor their deep rich culture. Their first years together, they lived in the housing provided by the dairy farm. But every year, without fail, my father came down with pneumonia. The cold, drafty dairy barns took their toll. Still, no matter how sick he got, he showed up. He needed the money. He refused to let his boss down.

Until one day, he couldn't.

The doctor gave him a final warning: "You have to find another line of work. Your body can't take this anymore."

Just when he had finally found stability, respect, and a sense of belonging, he had to start over – again.

I often wonder if his knack for getting pneumonia had something to do with the injuries from his fall years earlier. He never asked. Maybe it was best not to know. It wouldn't have changed the outcome.

With no choice but to pivot, he turned to construction. Another new skill set. Another unfamiliar world. Another place where he had to prove himself and earn respect. A few years in, he realized something:

This was honest work and the money was decent, but it wasn't his calling.

After grueling days on the construction site, he started his own side business – tending to people's yards at night. Although it was exhausting, he didn't care. He knew that his true path to the American Dream was to be his own boss, to build something that belonged to him.

But life had its own way of testing his resolve. One day, while working in a trench, waiting for a massive pipe to be laid down, disaster struck. The pipe was heavier than expected, and the supporters couldn't hold their ground. In a split second, instinct kicked in. He managed to yank his body out of harm's way, but not fast enough to save his hands – specifically, his thumb. The crushing weight was unforgiving.

During his recovery, unable to return to construction with winter layoffs looming, he found himself in desperate need of income to support his wife and daughter, my sister. That's when he secured part-time work at the Ormsby House, prepping and assisting in the kitchen. The job was a lifeline, and he was deeply grateful to the Basque man who had given him the opportunity. Every day, he showed up with determination – slicing vegetables, cutting meat, doing whatever was needed. But the walls felt like they were closing in. The confinement, the repetitive tasks, the absence of open skies – it gnawed at him. He felt trapped, caged by the very walls that provided him shelter.

Even while enduring that frustration, a fire burned brighter. Discomfort brought clarity. He realized he wasn't meant for the monotony of indoor routines; his spirit thrived in the open, under the vast Nevada skies, with the earth beneath his feet and the freedom to create.

This was his first taste of the deeper meaning behind entrepreneurship. It wasn't just about earning a living – it was about purpose, fulfillment, and the "why" that drove him. Change, uncomfortable as it was, became the catalyst for his transformation.

The following spring, when his construction job resumed, the company required out-of-town work. If he wanted to keep his job, he'd have to travel – but he didn't want to. He wanted to be home every night with his family. That realization was the final push. As he healed and regained his full physical strength, he took the risk. He made the leap. He left both construction and the confines of the kitchen behind to go all in on his landscaping and gardening business in Reno, Nevada.

A dream built from nothing. A future created by sheer will.

This change marked a turning point, a great leap toward his life's aspirations.

Like my father, change was nothing new to me. Maybe, in some crazy way, I even welcomed it. Discomfort meant growth, challenge, and learning.

But this time, change hadn't been on my terms.

A torn ACL and the looming reconstruction surgery meant my soccer dreams were on hold. I made the difficult decision to return home to have the surgery and rehab, knowing I could rely on my parents to help me through it. But I wasn't ready to leave Santa Rosa. I loved my teammates, friends, and school. In my mind, I was supposed to be "moving forward" – transferring to a new school, making new friends, and playing the game I loved.

This wasn't part of the plan. And I didn't embrace it. But if I had to do it, I was going to do it my way. I became obsessed with being the fastest-rehabbed ACL reconstruction patient in history. It was my new challenge, my new goal.

Being back home was hard. Other than family, I had no real connections. School felt like something I was just getting through. I told myself I was staying on track so I could transfer, but as the weeks turned into months, doubt crept in.

Could I ever be as good as I was before? Would I work hard just to lose it all again?

Instead of facing that fear, I quit first.

I walked away from soccer. And in doing so, I completely shifted my academic path. I was a year and a half away from a biology degree, but suddenly, I started looking for something different – something that felt possible.

At first, I thought I was starting over. But in reality, I was building on everything I had already learned - about discipline, resilience, and what it means to fight for something when no one else is watching.

That season, that injury, that moment of walking away, it all taught me something I couldn't have learned any other way. That persistence isn't just about holding on. It's about choosing to rise again after the thing you love breaks your heart. It's about adapting, even when the path looks nothing like you imagined.

And when I look back, whether it's my father on a mountainside with a flock, on a field chasing a ball, or in a business trying to build something real, the game is always the same. The world doesn't hand you success. You have to show up, take the hits, and decide - again and again - that you're still in it.

That's when I remembered a summer mentorship I had done in high school with someone in the field of forensics. He had been a huge inspiration to me for years. The work fascinated me. It was a puzzle – science, evidence, truth. It felt like the right path. I accepted my first full-time position as a forensic technician while finishing up that last year of college.

I pressed forward with my education, and during this last year of school, I happened to meet my husband, also at a Basque event like my parents met. Eight months later we were married, one month before I finally graduated from University. Neither of us set out to marry someone Basque, but from the very beginning, we just *got* each other. We came from the same traditions, spoke the same unspoken language, and shared a deep-rooted culture passed down through generations. We were both, by blood and ancestry, 100% Basque.

During our first years of marriage and having our first child - our daughter Kattalin - I enjoyed the work collecting evidence and processing crime scenes for the Sheriff's Department in the neighboring town. The work was intense, but it was meaningful.

And then everything changed again.

After having my second child - our son, Andoni - I realized this career wasn't built for the kind of mother I wanted to be. Crime didn't happen during convenient hours, and I was constantly missing time with my family. Worse, the job was making me jaded. Seeing the aftermath of crime every day, carrying those images into my sleep… it took a toll. It was lonely work. And I loved people – especially those who were alive.

There were scenes etched into my memory, haunting me long after the cases were closed. Like the day we were called out to a beautiful home with a picture-perfect yard, where the CFO of a very lucrative business had taken his own life, his wife in the adjacent room. The fear frozen on his lifeless face was something I saw in my sleep for weeks. The thought of him giving up everything – his life, relationships, and future – clung to me. As I meticulously collected evidence, I felt the weight of my own absence at home, missing out on the things that mattered most. I couldn't shake the realization of how lucky I was to still have my life, my family, my moments – luxuries that he no longer had.

And then there was the older woman, found dead in the sweltering heat of July. She had been gone for months before a neighbor finally made the call. Her body was partially mummified, maggots thriving where decay had taken hold. The stench was overwhelming, a putrid reminder of neglect and loneliness that clung to my skin and seeped into my pores. I spent more than 20 hours on that scene, documenting, collecting, existing in the midst of her final, undignified chapter. Despite showering and changing before heading home, the smell followed me. My husband recoiled when I walked through the door, unable to bear the lingering scent of death. Even after another shower, the image of her frail, forgotten body haunted me – a woman who had been left to die alone in a house she once shared with family too lost in their own struggles to care.

Witnessing the worst of humanity, the aftermath of despair, and the fragility of life eroded pieces of me. I couldn't help but fathom the waste of potential, the lives cut short, the missed chances for purpose and peace. It was in those dark reflections that clarity emerged: This job was devouring parts of me that I needed to keep whole. I wanted to be present, to cherish the fleeting, beautiful moments with my family – to love the living, not just investigate the lost.

It was time to pivot, again.

I made the decision to go back to school and earn my master's degree. My goal was to teach science, including forensics, so I could stay connected to the science I loved, but in a way that offered more balance. My husband, Mikel, had been a teacher for years and spoke often about the joy of connecting with students, sharing knowledge, and helping them find their path. The more I explored the idea, the more clearly I could see myself in that role. But there was one major challenge: in order to make this transition work, I had to find a way to replace my forensic salary - while also being a present mom and wife and carving out time and having flexibility to attend school.

So I bought a business.

In my mind, it was the perfect solution. Flexibility. A salary. Time with family.

Except… it was the wrong business. We had no idea what we were getting into..

My husband was on board with buying a business, knowing that it would be one that I operated. He would continue his career path in education while helping me when possible behind the scenes. We bought an independently owned mailbox and shipping business from a guy who, as it turned out, had been running some seriously shady operations behind the scenes. Being new and inexperienced, we didn't even know the right questions to ask during the buying process. On paper, everything looked perfect, but reality told a different story.

Two weeks in, it hit me like a freight train: Something wasn't right.

The numbers he had shown us? Impossible to achieve by doing things ethically and legally. And I wasn't about to compromise my integrity just to make it work.

So my husband and I knew we had to do something drastic and fast; our life savings, our home, and our security was on the line. We had to revamp and rebuild this business the right way and do whatever it took to make it work. Selling it for a profit had been the original plan, but now survival was the only priority.

I knew how to hustle; sports had taught me that. And if I could push through injuries, setbacks, and doubts on the field, I could figure this out too.

Back then, there was no social media, no digital marketing, no fancy automation. What did I have? A printer, some paper, and two feet willing to hit the pavement with a lot of energy to let people know we existed and how we could help them.

We designed the brochures and business cards ourselves. I knocked on business doors, introduced myself to everyone who would listen, and made it my mission to turn this business into something real, something sustainable, and something we could be proud of.

It took time. It took grit. It took every ounce of energy and faith we had.

But we scaled that business.

We made our payments, gained momentum, and day by day, it got a little easier. It gave me the chance to go back to school, be present for my kids, and contribute financially to our family.

And when the time was right, we sold that business for a profit. That sale paid for my Master's degree and gave us a little more for savings. And when I got my teaching job, I thought I had finally reached my destination. But looking back, that business wasn't just about making money or covering tuition. It was my first real experience as an entrepreneur.

My father had experienced change in ways I couldn't fully grasp when I was young. He had to reinvent himself, take risks, and make difficult decisions to create a better life. And whether I realized it or not, I was following the same path.

Life and business are a series of choices. Stay comfortable in a situation that isn't working, even if it drains you. Or take a risk, push through discomfort, and build something better. I could have stayed in my forensics job, just like so many entrepreneurs stay stuck in a business that no longer serves them. I could have kept missing out on family moments, telling myself, "This is just how it is." But I made a choice.

Every entrepreneur who has a business that is struggling faces the same decision: Will you keep moving along, barely getting by? Or will you tear it down and rebuild – even when it's uncomfortable?

At the end of the day, growth doesn't happen in comfort. There's a saying: "Growth happens at the edge of your comfort zone." The real breakthroughs come when you decide to push through.

Growth doesn't happen in comfort…
The real breakthroughs come when
you decide to push through.

Hazkundea ez da erosotasunean gertatzen…
Benetako aurrerapenak aurrera egitea
erabakitzen duzunean datoz.

CHAPTER 6

The Courage to Create Your Own Path: Innovation, Resourcefulness, and the Power of Failure

For my father, starting his side business – maintaining yards and offering gardening services in the evenings and on weekends – became a full-fledged thriving business. With every new client, he built not only a business but also a dream. The move to Reno made sense; it was better for business, brought my mom back to her hometown and closer to her family, and kept my father near my uncles who had also come to America, all of whom had settled in the Gardnerville/Reno area.

By the time I was born, my father had established himself as a full-time entrepreneur, running his gardening and landscaping business with passion, grit, and joy. Through relentless effort, he planted the seeds of a legacy, one rooted in hard work and determination – a legacy that shaped my life as I grew up.

He built his business one client at a time, often beginning his days before the sun rose and finishing only when the job met his exacting standards. For him, work wasn't just about earning a living; it was an expression of respect – for himself, his clients, and the life he was creating for his family.

My father started his gardening business with virtually no resources and very little money. He had a vision, a will, and a creative mind. Resourcefulness became his superpower, along with his ability to innovate something out of nothing. When he couldn't afford the right accessories for his truck or the right trailer to haul tools and debris, he didn't see a problem – he saw a challenge. Armed with creativity and elbow grease, he built his own "perfect" equipment. His truck had tall racks to secure grass and branches, a screen to protect the back window, and even a hydraulic dump bed. This was back in the '80s when no one had a dump bed on their '82 Chevy truck. The trailer? A marvel of organization, complete with compartments for every tool imaginable and a water system to keep the crew hydrated during scorching summers. It wasn't just functional; it was a rolling testament to his ingenuity.

He sharpened and fixed most of his equipment himself, unless he absolutely couldn't, in which case my mom would haul it into the lawnmower shop during her lunch hour. After work, we'd swing by to pick it up, and the routine would continue. I loved that lawnmower shop. It smelled of grease, fresh grass trimmings, and dirt. A bell sat on the counter, tempting me during every visit. Even if the owners were right there, I couldn't resist ringing it. My mom, of course, shot me the "mom eyes" for disrupting the silence with a playful grab at attention, but all I felt was joy. If the bell wasn't meant to be rung, why put it on the counter?

Through the years, my father's resourcefulness and innovation solved so many problems. But not every solution was a triumph. Some were... let's call them learning experiences. Like the time he decided to speed up the process of drying peppers to make his homemade cayenne pepper powder.

My father had grown up without electricity, in a farmhouse shared with animals and a dozen family members. When the microwave entered our lives, it was as if magic had arrived. It heated and cooked food in just minutes! One day, to avoid the months-long wait for peppers to dry, he had an epiphany: Why not use the microwave? He had learned early on that time was valuable and efficiency was key to accomplishing what needed to be done each day to achieve success. The peppers were stuffed into the microwave and the time punched in. Minutes later, the house was engulfed in a potent cloud of what can only be described as homemade pepper spray.

It was a weekday so all the grandchildren were at the house with their grandparents - Mom used to watch the kids when we were at work. As grandparents and grandkids evacuated, coughing and rubbing burning eyes, my mother was furious. She prided herself on keeping the kids safe and maintaining order in the beautiful chaos of life. But that day, the house turned into a pepper spray gas chamber, leaving everyone fleeing like it was a fire drill gone wrong.

My father, however, was unfazed. When we arrived to pick up the kids, standing on the porch, he calmly explained that he believed it was a good idea. "How could I have known it would turn out like this?" he stated. And then, as if the moment of disaster never happened, he announced that he would find another way. Failure wasn't an end for him; it was simply a redirection. The only lesson he took away? The microwave would henceforth be used solely for heating water and oatmeal.

Years later, I found myself in a situation that echoed his journey in many ways, facing a leap into the unknown. Moving to a new town – no connections, no friends, and no opportunities in the teaching career I had worked so hard to build – felt like starting over. And in many ways, it was.

I was devastated that there were no teaching positions, but deep down, I knew I couldn't just wait for one to appear. Hustle and work were my outlets; I very much enjoyed working. Sitting around with nothing to do while battling loneliness in a new place was a recipe for disaster. The only bright spots were getting to drop off and pick up my kids from school – something my mom had always done for me in Reno while I worked. But the hours in between? They felt empty.

I had a choice: I could wait around for a job to find me, or I could go find one. So I began researching opportunities I could do from home to maintain flexibility for my children. Consulting caught my interest. I had done some educational consulting work on the side while teaching. I loved business and franchise consulting seemed like an exciting way to learn about different franchise opportunities while helping potential buyers make informed decisions.

So I leaped. I invested my hard-earned savings into a franchise consulting business. A week into the two-week training, I realized I had made a huge mistake. Franchise consulting, as it turned out, wasn't about serving people in the way I thought I would by getting them into their very own businesses. Instead, it was solely about making sales. And I absolutely sucked at cold calling and pushy sales tactics. To truly be successful with their trained methods, you had to be good at both.

Sales, in this format, felt icky. My approach to business had always been personal: sharing my story, solving a problem, and genuinely helping people with my products and services. But this? This to me felt like it was about closing deals and moving on. My heart wasn't in it and my results reflected that. When I finally made a few sales, I lost sleep worrying about the people who bought them, hoping they weren't making a mistake. I dreaded every day of it and it showed in my "success" or lack thereof.

Months passed and still no hopeful teaching opportunities emerged, and I felt stuck doing a job I hated. I longed for connection. I longed to belong to a community and do work I enjoyed.

One specific day stands out. I was sitting at my desk, staring at my computer, my fingers hovering over the keyboard, dreading yet another round of cold calls. My heart felt heavy, my chest tight, and my stomach twisted with anxiety. The thought of calling those numbers filled me with dread. Questions raced through my mind: *Why am I doing this? Is this really what I worked so hard for?* The silence in the room was deafening, broken only by the faint hum of the computer. That was the day the weight of failure hit me the hardest.

The turning point came one ordinary afternoon. I caught my reflection in the dark screen of my computer and, for a moment, I didn't recognize the person staring back. I looked tired, defeated, and lost. That reflection was my wakeup call. It was time to pivot – to pick myself up and figure out what was next. Failure didn't have to be final; and deep down, I knew I was meant for something different. I just needed to figure out what that was.

Entrepreneurship wasn't new to me. And while I technically owned my own franchise consulting business, it wasn't the kind of business I had grown up admiring and it wasn't anything like my first business. When I bought my first business, I knew it would be hard. But I also knew that the struggle would be worth it, and it was. Building something of my own and experiencing the success it brought wasn't just rewarding – it was life-changing. The key was figuring out how to achieve this again doing something I loved which also allowed me to be the mom I wanted to be. That was non-negotiable. I envisioned building a business that allowed me to find belonging in this new community, make a positive impact, and build something meaningful, something with purpose. My father had built a legacy, something meaningful, something that filled him with purpose and joy, and that was the kind of business I knew I needed to find.

Loneliness wasn't just an occasional feeling; it was a constant, heavy companion that settled into the spaces within and between my days. I remember walking into a bustling coffee shop after dropping my youngest off at school, the rich aroma of freshly brewed coffee swirling with the warmth of cinnamon and vanilla. The air buzzed with the laughter of friends reunited, the soft clinking of cups creating a rhythm that felt foreign to me. I stood there, wrapped in the invisible cloak of isolation, watching a world that seemed to spin effortlessly without me. Everyone had someone. Everyone belonged.

I ordered my coffee, my voice a soft murmur, and found refuge at a small corner table. I stared out the window, the blur of passing faces a stark reminder of the connections I craved but couldn't find. The voices in my head grew louder than the crowd around me: *You don't fit in. You'll never find your place here. What were you thinking?* The weight of those words pressed and tightened around my chest. But somewhere beneath the noise, a fragile whisper surfaced: *Keep going. You're stronger than this.*

That whisper became my anchor.

So with lessons learned and my heart set on creating something that mattered, I set out to forge my way forward – failure, lessons, innovation, and all. Finally, I made the choice to walk away from the franchise consulting business that didn't work. I decided to step forward, take a risk, and create something better.

And that's how I found myself standing in the middle of a restaurant, ready to start again on my third business venture.

This decision wasn't easy. I wrestled with it for months, weighed down by doubts. My husband who had his own career as a Principal of a school was not on board with a business, especially not a restaurant business. He lovingly and candidly told me that he would be here to support me, but he had no intention of working the business. I had no network, no experience, and no guarantees. Sure, I'd waitressed in college, but I'd never stepped foot in a kitchen as anything more than a server. Nor had I managed a restaurant, for that matter. Growing up, though, the kitchen was the heart of our home. Cooking was how we pitched in, and my mom and sister were incredible cooks. I loved the warmth of hospitality, the way food brought people together and created lasting memories.

Food was more than a love language; it was the connector of all things for me, such as friends, culture, traditions, and conversations. Every great story was told around the table. But I had no idea what any of it looked like from the other side – owning a food business. Every rational argument said, "Don't do it." But my gut? My gut told me this was the way forward. A chance to rebuild. To find connection. To serve a purpose when I felt so lost and alone.

With lessons etched into the fabric of my heart, I set out to create something more than just a business. Owning a restaurant wasn't about profits or transactions; it was about finding purpose when I felt lost. It became my sanctuary, a space where I could pour my longing for connection into every dish, every detail. It was proof that even in the depths of loneliness, you can build bridges – to others, to a community, and back to yourself. It was about creating a place that mattered, a place that held meaning beyond its walls. A space where I could heal, grow, make an impact, build a legacy, and most importantly, be the mom I longed to be – present, fulfilled, and connected.

My father's challenges were like mountains – steep, treacherous, and life-defining. Mine, though smaller, still tested me in ways I had never imagined. I was an outsider in an unfamiliar industry, competing against businesses that had been here for decades. I had no background in restaurants, no deep pockets, no safety net. But in true Basque spirit, I embraced the paradox: stay humble, stay under the radar – but dream big. I was willing to bet on myself and determined to turn my vision into reality. I was choosing to bounce back from a failed effort by trying again. I wasn't just taking another risk; I was taking a bigger one. A financial leap that made my stomach turn. But deep down, I knew

– the little girl who had once played restaurant in her grandfather's backyard knew – this was the right risk.

So I stepped into the unknown and kept showing up. Every single day.

I heard the doubts, felt the resistance, and carried the weight of uncertainty. But I refused to let outside voices dictate my path. This wasn't about blind confidence; it was about purpose. I knew exactly why I was doing this, and that sense of clarity made every discomfort, every challenge, worth it.

My husband who had originally told me I was on my own in this crazy restaurant adventure, ended up helping me in the background with the tech, construction, creativity and weekly special creations throughout our journey. I didn't have the luxury of a big budget – just a shoestring and the determination to make it stretch. But that limitation became a hidden gift. When you have no choice but to make it work, resourcefulness and innovation aren't optional; they become your superpowers. You learn to stretch a dollar further than you ever imagined. You discover how to create something meaningful, something remarkable, with almost nothing.

And in those moments of scrappy creativity and relentless problem-solving, I finally understood the true source of my father's strength. It wasn't just in what he built, but in how he built it – with grit, ingenuity, and an unwavering belief that where there's a will, there's always a way.

I know people thought I was crazy. Owning a restaurant while maintaining a close, healthy relationship with my kids and my husband? Unheard of. But at the core of every decision, I asked myself one simple, grounding question: *Does this align with what matters most – my family?* Every choice I made was filtered through the lens of knowing the kind of life I wanted to create for my children and share with family. Their well-being, our connection, and the time we shared were non-negotiable. No business goal was ever worth more than the people who held my heart.

Despite the skepticism, I pressed on. I didn't see challenges as roadblocks; I saw them as fuel. Others couldn't see my vision, but that belief anchored me. The doubt didn't break me – it made me work smarter, push harder, and stay focused.

Looking back, I see it clearly. Sheepherding and business ownership don't seem connected, but they are. My father's long, grueling days in the high desert weren't just about survival; they were about patience, resilience, and solitude. He learned that success doesn't happen in the spotlight – it happens in the quiet, unseen effort.

That's the same foundation I built my restaurant business on.

Watching my father, I didn't just learn how to work hard, I learned how to reinvent. How to turn obstacles into opportunities. How to carve out a path when none seemed to exist.

And that's what business really is. It's not about having all the answers upfront; it's about solving problems as you go. It's about seeing limitations not as roadblocks but as opportunities to innovate. What if a lack of funding wasn't an excuse to quit, but an invitation to be more creative? What if uncertainty wasn't something to fear, but something to navigate with curiosity?

I think about that a lot.

How many of us let fear stop us from taking the risk we know deep down we need to take?

How often do we wait for the perfect moment, the perfect plan, the perfect guarantee – when in reality, the path is built when we step forward before we are even ready?

What would happen if, instead of waiting, we always chose to bet on ourselves?

And sometimes, it comes down to this:
You either adapt and evolve,
or you risk being left behind.

Eta batzuetan, honetara iristen da kontua:
edo egokitu eta eboluzionatu egiten duzu,
edo atzean geratzeko arriskua duzu.

CHAPTER 7

Adapt or Get Left Behind: The Role of Curiosity in Business Evolution

Growing up in an immigrant household, adaptation wasn't just something we did – it was how we survived. Curiosity was our secret weapon, the force that kept us moving forward, figuring things out, and showing up better each day. Life was a delicate dance between holding on to the familiarity of our Basque culture and learning how to navigate the exciting American way. At home, we lived one foot in the old world and one foot in the new, constantly shifting between cultures, expectations, and definitions of success.

Our home smelled of homemade vegetable and cabbage soup, garlic sizzling in olive oil with potatoes, lamb baking in the oven or steaks coming off the barbeque, and the faint, earthy aroma of red wine that my father sipped with dinner after long days of work. Family gatherings were filled with the sounds of laughter and Euskera (our Basque language), layered over the rhythmic beat of the accordion squeezing out traditional Basque music. Tables overflowed with plates of chorizo, jamon, lamb, dry jack cheese, fresh French bread, salad, homemade fried patatas, and more. Yet, outside our doors, the world moved to a different rhythm – hamburgers and hotdogs, ball games, and old-fashioned American music. Over time, these differences didn't just coexist – they blended, creating a rich tapestry that shaped my identity.

My father, despite having no more than a third-grade education, possessed a remarkable intelligence that went far beyond formal schooling. He never stopped learning. Education to him was the ticket to a better life, and he made sure we knew it. "Go to school, get a good education, get a good job," he'd say, believing that a formal education would give us the stability and opportunities he never had. Sometimes, I wonder if he saw his lack of formal education as a weakness. But looking back, I realize his true strength – and the lessons he instilled in us – had nothing to do with a classroom. He taught us resilience, the power of relentless curiosity, and the skill of figuring things out, no matter the circumstances. Those lessons weren't found in textbooks; they were learned through experience, determination, and the refusal to let uncertainty stand in the way. Learning isn't just about books or degrees; it's about asking the right questions, staying curious, and adapting to whatever life throws your way.

My father embodied this mindset. He never let what he didn't know hold him back. If he saw something unfamiliar – a machine, a tool, a new way of doing business – he wouldn't just ignore it. He'd stop, watch, ask questions, and gather every bit of knowledge he could. Curiosity fueled his survival, and survival demanded adaptation.

We saw this in action all the time as kids. To him, every problem had a solution. You just had to be willing to find it.

And then there was the skunk.

My father raised chickens for eggs. One summer, my dad noticed something was stealing his baby chicks. At first, it was just a few, but soon, several more had vanished. Something was hunting them, and my dad was determined to find out what.

For weeks, he tracked footprints in the dirt, examined the coop, and studied the land around it. He noticed faint disturbances near a culvert at the edge of the property. A predator was living there. He thought he knew what type of animal but he wasn't completely sure.

One day, he decided to put his theory to the test. He asked my mom and my 4-year-old son to stand at one end of the culvert while he fired up his high-powered leaf blower at the other. "Just let me know if anything comes out," he said casually, leaving out one tiny detail....

The skunk.

Seconds later, a black-and-white blur shot out of the culvert, charging straight toward my mom and son.

My mom let out a screech, grabbed my son, and took off running while yelling, "It's a SKUNK!"

From his spot at the other end, my dad grinned. "How many?" he asked.

Mom, with a boost of adrenaline and irritation, shot him a glare. "How many?! I didn't stop to count. I ran before we got sprayed." And then she put the pieces together and asked him if he knew it was a skunk.

His eyes twinkled as he shrugged, completely unfazed. "I was pretty sure, but not completely sure," he admitted.

Mom was less than impressed. "And you didn't think we should know that?!"

He laughed and just answered "Well, how else was I going to know for sure it was a skunk and it was out unless I had a witness?"

Problem solved.

He screened off the ends of the culvert, ensuring no skunks could make a home there again. But he also understood something deeper – predators change, threats evolve, and solutions must adapt. That's when he built a stronger coop, a taller fence, and implemented a habit of locking the chickens in every night. Because solving one problem wasn't enough; he had to think ahead.

It wasn't just about getting rid of the skunk. It was about adapting to prevent the next challenge.

And that was my dad's philosophy – whether in life, business, or skunk evictions.

You don't need to know everything, you just need to stay curious enough to figure it out.

As a kid, curiosity was both my greatest teacher and my fastest ticket to trouble. Asking "Why?" helped me grow and learn, but wondering, "What would happen if…?" often landed me in situations that tested the limits of what was considered "acceptable" behavior.

Take my fascination with bugs. I didn't just want to see them, I wanted to study them. Whenever I found a freshly dead insect or a worm that had dried out on the pavement after a summer rain, I'd collect them and carefully arrange them on my dresser. It was my own little science experiment, my curiosity-fueled lab.

My mother, however, saw things a little differently. A very clean and organized woman, she would walk into my room only to find an assortment of dried bugs and worms proudly displayed, waiting for me to analyze them, track their changes, and – in my mind – unlock the mysteries of nature. Her reaction? Horrified. Every. Single. Time.

And every time, I got in trouble. Not only would I have to clean my room from top to bottom, but she also worried about the inevitable leftover dirt, bug parts, or whatever unintentional science residue might remain. But curiosity wasn't something I could turn off. And it didn't stop at my bedroom experiments.

Once a month or so, our family would go out to eat at a Mexican restaurant, a rare treat. The food was great but, for me, the most fascinating thing about the place was the massive gong by the host stand.

Every time we walked in, it called to me.

It just sat there – silent, waiting. The mallet always hung beside it, yet I had never once seen anyone strike it. And that made me wonder... How loud was it? Would it sound as deep and thunderous as it did on TV?

One evening, curiosity won.

We had just been called for our table. As we slowly followed the host, we passed by the gong, and for the first time, I was close enough to reach the mallet.

I swung.

The deep, resounding crash of the gong filled the entire restaurant. Conversation stopped. Diners turned. And at that moment, our family – who prided ourselves on flying under the radar – became the center of attention.

My mother's face turned red on the spot. Her "mom eyes" locked onto me, an unspoken promise that I was absolutely in for it later.

But my father? He just laughed under his breath, shaking his head with that familiar twinkle in his eye. He leaned in and, in the most understated way, whispered, "Oh, you are so curious."

It was both a compliment and a warning. He wasn't going to step on my mother's authority, but in his own way, he was cheering me on.

Looking back, I realize that curiosity, even when it got me in trouble, was never something I needed to suppress. It was a driving force – one that would later shape the way I learned, adapted, and approached every challenge in business and in life.

My natural curiosity and ability to adapt were the anchors that helped me navigate the unpredictable tides of the restaurant industry. Every day presented a new challenge – a missing ingredient from a supplier, an unexpected catering order that needed to be delivered on short notice, or equipment deciding to break down on the busiest day of the year. In those moments, survival wasn't about having all the answers; it was about staying curious enough to find them.

Running a restaurant taught me that business isn't just about solving problems; it's about adapting when faced with the unexpected. It's about looking at what's right in front of you, asking the right questions, and figuring out how to move forward even when the path isn't clear. Curiosity wasn't just a trait I had; it was the tool I used to keep my business afloat.

As the restaurant gained momentum, I made a conscious choice to prepare for the "maybe someday" and the "just in case for tomorrow." I increased the percentage I saved from profits, stayed strategic about expenses, scrutinized the cost of goods, and cut out the "extras" we didn't really need to run the business. I kept wearing multiple hats, not because I had to, but because it allowed me to save more for that "maybe someday" rainy day.

But beyond the business, my heart was always anchored at home. My days weren't just about managing orders, leading a team, or solving the next business challenge. They were also about being present for my kids. Mornings often started way before dawn, especially on catering days. As the catering side of the business grew, so did the demands: 400 breakfast burritos ready by 5:00 am or a full breakfast for 300 people by 6:00 am. And it didn't stop there. The same day would roll right into preparing hundreds of boxed lunches or sandwich platters with sides for 200 people – all prepped, packed, and out the door by 11:30 am.

Those days were exhilarating, fueled by adrenaline and purpose. Planning and strategy became my constant companions. In the early days of my business, mornings were a delicate dance of juggling responsibilities. My husband would drop off our daughter on his way to work, then bring our son to me at the restaurant before starting his own day. It wasn't unusual for me to arrive at the restaurant before dawn to organize, prep, and get ahead of the rush. So when my husband would drop off our son, I'd pause at 8:00 am, hustle to get our son to school, then drive back to work.

Getting to the restaurant in the wee hours of morning was never a sacrifice because I knew my "why" and my purpose, and I also made the choice to go into work early because it allowed me to stay aligned with what mattered most in my life: showing up and being a present mom. By 1:45 pm, I'd shift gears completely – leaving to pick up my kids from school, transitioning from business owner to mom. Afternoons were sacred – reserved for school pickups, sports practices, homework sessions, family dinners, and bedtime routines. Despite the chaos, those moments grounded me, reminding me of my "why." I was fortunate to live both roles fully, finding fulfillment in each.

As our team grew from four to 23, my leadership had to evolve. In the beginning, I managed with instinct, fueled by passion and a hands-on approach. But as the business expanded, I faced new challenges. More moving parts, more orders, more expenses, more opportunities to adapt. I stayed curious: *Where is there a need we can fill? How can we do better? How do I lead a team with high expectations while showing genuine appreciation for their contributions?* Balancing the needs of the business with empathy for every single employee I cared about was one of the hardest lessons I had to learn. I doubted myself, questioning whether I was being too harsh or too lenient. Over time, I realized that leadership isn't about having all the answers or being liked all the time. It's about making tough decisions with integrity, leading with both heart and clarity.

Even as the business grew, I never got complacent. I paid attention to what others in the industry were doing – whether it was during trips out of town or late-night deep dives into industry trends online. I was always searching for better ways, new approaches, different strategies that could give us an edge. I didn't know that "tomorrow" would be March, 2020—the month the pandemic flipped our world upside down.

Because of the foundation I'd built – financially, emotionally, and mentally – I was more prepared than I realized. The pandemic tested that mindset harder than anything I'd ever faced. I remember sitting alone one day in the dim light of my closed restaurant. The chairs were stacked, the hum of the kitchen silenced. The emptiness was deafening. A lump formed in my throat as I stared at the vacant tables, wondering if this was the end of everything I had built. Fear crept in – not just for the business, but for my team, my family, our future.

But amid the uncertainty, a quiet voice inside whispered, *What can you do right now?* That question became my anchor. It wasn't about having all the answers; it was about staying curious enough to find the next step.

The first few months were brutal. My team members weren't just employees; they represented my business family. One day, we needed every single person to keep things running like a well-oiled machine. The next, there was no work, no certainty, no guarantees.

We had the hard conversation with them: "They say it'll be a couple of weeks, but what if it's longer?" Some team members chose to leave, but most wanted to stay, either because they loved the work or needed the income. I felt a deep responsibility to figure it out and keep them employed, even when business had come to a screeching halt.

Weeks turned into a month, and I knew that if we didn't pivot, I wouldn't be able to keep them at all.

Yet, amid the unknown, I felt something unexpected: gratitude. From day one, I had saved during the good months, knowing unpredictability was inevitable. I kept expenses steady, monitored costs relentlessly, and let profits grow – not just for success, but for survival.

When the pandemic hit, everything changed overnight. Our loyal restaurant following couldn't walk through our doors, and our booming catering business came to an abrupt halt. Curiosity became my lifeline. How could we continue doing business and offering our catering safely? We pivoted – individually packaged lunches delivered to sites where people could pick them up, new bidding strategies, and streamlined delivery operations. Every day brought new rules, but we kept asking questions, stayed flexible, and adapted. And we made it through.

All along, the real game of business was happening: refining systems, making operations more efficient, and always having a plan. The challenge in doing all of this was actually the fun part. It was constant adaptation to just keep getting better.

During the pandemic, I was forced to adapt to keep the business humming and adapting needed to be fast. I had saved for rainy days, but this storm wasn't passing. The massive pivot was the only way forward if we were going to come out thriving. That's what adaptation is really all about. In business, success doesn't come from having all the answers. It comes from being willing to learn, evolve, and take action even when you're unsure.

When it comes down to it, life isn't about having a perfect plan, and neither is finding success in business. We show up as who we think we need to be, do what we think we should do, and grow the way we think we're supposed to. But if we stay curious – if we ask "What if?" and "Why not?" – we open ourselves to growth we never imagined.

The people who succeed in business aren't always the smartest or the most experienced; they're the owners who are willing to learn, evolve, and take action even when they don't know what the future holds.

So as you reflect on your own business, ask yourself:

- *Where have you been resistant to change because it felt too uncertain?*

- *What would happen if you approached challenges with curiosity instead of fear?*

- *How can you create systems that allow flexibility and growth, even when the unexpected happens?*

- *Are you asking the right questions to uncover hidden opportunities in your business?*

When it comes down to it, life isn't a straight line or a perfectly laid-out plan. We often show up each day trying to be who we think we should be, doing what we believe we're supposed to do, and chasing growth the way we think it's meant to happen. But as we continue to grow and remain curious, we eventually realize that maybe it's not about following a predetermined path. Maybe it's about pausing long enough to ask ourselves: *What if there's another way?* Maybe growth isn't about having all the answers, but rather it's about staying open to new possibilities, new lessons, and new ways of being. It's in that space – where curiosity meets courage – that true transformation happens.

And sometimes, it comes down to this: You either adapt and evolve, or you risk being left behind.

And that's where hard work comes into play. Because curiosity without action is just daydreaming. Adaptation without effort is just wishful thinking. It's one thing to ask the questions, but it's the dedication, consistency, and relentless pursuit of progress that turns curiosity into meaningful action. It's the power of hard work – not just as a means to an end, but as a fundamental part of growth, success, and building a life and business that truly matter.

Hard work isn't just about endurance;
it's the catalyst for transformation.

Lan gogorra ez da erresistentzia kontua bakarrik;
eraldaketarako katalizatzailea ere bada.

CHAPTER 8

The Joy in Hard Work: Building Success with Purpose

In my family, hard work wasn't just something we talked about – it was the rhythm of life itself. Mornings often began before dawn, with the scent of fresh coffee mingling with the crisp, cool air from the open windows as my father pulled on his worn work boots, their leather softened by use. The sound of the kitchen door opening and slamming shut was our daily alarm clock, signaling that the day had begun. The kitchen would hum with activity as my mother prepared a hearty breakfast – fuel for the long day ahead. Outside, the animals waited to be fed, while the distant hum of a lawnmower became the soundtrack of our lives. The sharpened ones were loaded in the trailer along with the equipment and tools needed, ready for hands that knew them well. This wasn't just work; it was a way of being, a tradition carried through generations, stitched into the fabric of our family story. My father never sat us down to preach about the value of hard work; it was written in the calluses on his hands, etched into the lines of his face, and woven into the quiet strength of his resolve. It lived in the sacrifices he made without complaint, the early mornings, and the long days. For us, his daughters, hard work wasn't taught – it was absorbed, simply by watching him and my mom live it every single day.

My sister and I grew up immersed in this culture. We had chores, responsibilities, and expectations – tasks that might seem small to others were treated with purpose and pride in our household. My mom managed all the "inside jobs," while my dad ruled over everything outdoors. Together, my sister and I bridged both worlds: scrubbing bathrooms until they gleamed, helping prepare family meals, picking up every last scrap of evergreen trimmings after pruning bushes, and harvesting every green bean in the garden.

In our family, work wasn't done until it was done right. My parents were perfectly aligned in their belief that every task deserved our full effort, and sometimes, even our hobbies followed the same rules. My father not only taught us the value of hard work, he showed us the importance of excellence. He believed there was dignity in every job, no matter how humble, as long as it was done with care. It wasn't about getting credit. His pride came from within, rooted in the quiet satisfaction of knowing he had done his best.

But life wasn't all grind; it was also about joy. My father's lessons extended even to the hobbies he loved, like fishing. We'd head out by dawn, trekking through rugged trails and thick willows along the creeks of the Sierra Nevada Mountains, following the crystal-clear waters flowing from Lake Tahoe. When we asked, "Why not fish in the easy spots?" he'd simply say, "That's where everyone else goes, and the smart fish know it." Fishing wasn't just a pastime; it was a lesson in effort, patience, and respect – for both the process and the catch.

It was the same with our annual alfalfa haul, our mission to stock up on feed for the livestock through harsh winters. Every summer, we'd make trips to Carson Valley ranches, hauling truckloads of alfalfa bales. My mom drove the truck, my dad stacked the bales, and my sister and I hoisted them up one by one. The ride home was always a spectacle, our truck stacked high like something out of "The Beverly Hillbillies" – except instead of possessions, we had alfalfa. Unloading was just as labor-intensive, stacking each bale meticulously in the barn. There were easier ways to do it, but my dad insisted on our way – teaching us, through grit and sweat, the satisfaction of completing a tough job. And he always found a way to lighten the mood with jokes and stories.

We joked about "the Basque way," but it was more than just a phrase – it was a reflection of how deeply effort was ingrained in us, a badge of honor earned through perseverance. That same spirit defined my father's journey, shaping not only his life but the legacy he built for our family.

Looking back, my father's story is one of transformation, a journey from sheepherding to entrepreneurship, fueled by an unwavering determination to live the American Dream. I remember him sharing stories of long, solitary days spent in the high desert, tending to sheep with nothing but the vast sky above and the wind as his companions. Those moments taught him patience, resilience, and the value of quiet reflection. When he transitioned into running his own gardening and landscaping business, he carried those lessons with him.

I can still picture him meticulously planning his day at the crack of dawn, his hands rough from years of manual labor but steady with purpose. I'd often see him repairing equipment late into the evening, covered in dirt and sweat, with the faint smell of gasoline, yet his spirit never wavered. He had an innate belief that every challenge was an opportunity to learn and grow. Whether it was communicating with customers, managing crews, or ensuring that every blade of grass was perfectly trimmed, he approached each task with the same diligence and pride he had when watching over his flock.

He came to this country with little more than grit and the hope of building a better future for him and his family. Success wasn't handed down; it was earned through hard work, one backbreaking day at a time, shaped by both the rugged landscapes he once roamed and the thriving yards he later cultivated.

After almost 40 years of building a thriving gardening and landscaping business, my father retired, ready to embrace more freedom. He hoped to go fishing, play cards with friends, and spend time at home with the animals he loved and the expansive garden he tended with pride. His purpose had shifted. Now, it was time to enjoy the fruits of his years, time spent with less stress and more space for the people and passions that mattered most to him.

When my husband, children, and I moved to a new town, four hours from my family, their absence left a hole in my heart. My parents didn't visit often, and owning a restaurant while raising two children busy with school and sports left little time to travel to see them. I missed them deeply, especially my father's energy and zest for life, which always reminded me of the possibilities and beauty of owning your own business.

I remember standing in the bustling kitchen of my restaurant, the air thick with the aroma of sautéed garlic and the clatter of pots and pans. The clock ticked past 4:00 am, yet the adrenaline kept me going like I'd just arrived – preparing for the day's rush, reviewing catering orders, and scrubbing down the prep counter until it gleamed, ready to do the next task.

At that moment, as I thought about my childhood and all I had learned, I realized yet again that hard work is where ideas meet execution. It's the bridge between what you imagine and what you achieve. While curiosity sparks the questions and adaptation guides the path, it's hard work that pushes you to take the next step – even when it's uncomfortable, even when it's tough. It's not about grinding endlessly without purpose; it's about showing up with intention, doing the work that matters, and committing to the process, even when results aren't immediate. Like the time I spent hours perfecting a single recipe until it was just right – not for applause, but for the satisfaction of knowing I gave it my best.

Hard work is the engine that transforms dreams into reality, and without it, even the best ideas remain just that – ideas. And I was so grateful that I was brought up in a home that embraced the ideals of giving your best effort and working at what you really want to achieve.

Owning that restaurant was so much more than making money. It was about connection, purpose, perpetuating my Basque culture, and leaving a legacy in a place where I often felt alone. I still remember the early mornings that bled into long days, the jangle of pots and pans mingling with laughter from the kitchen, and the warmth of conversations among employees and customers that left me smiling and feeling at home. There were mornings when I'd arrive before the sun had risen, the scent of freshly baked cookies filling the kitchen, a quiet promise of the day's potential. Some nights, I'd sit alone at home, family in bed, house quiet, and I would think about the day – what could have been better, what went really well, exhaustion tugging at my bones but pride swelling in my chest.

It wasn't always easy. There were moments when the weight of responsibility felt overwhelming, like when unforeseen staff shortages meant I was cooking on the line, taking orders, and washing dishes all in one day. The crazy days when it felt like we were chasing our tail all day, the unexpected happened, and it was just about survival to get through the day. Or the quiet days during the pandemic when customers were few and doubt crept in, questioning whether it was all worth it. But it was in those quiet, challenging moments that I found my purpose. I'd think of my father's relentless dedication, the way he met each day with determination, and I'd remind myself why I started.

Part of that choice was to teach my children the importance of hard work and the belief in possibilities – what you can create if you decide it's what you truly want. I could never have built that business without the work ethic embedded in my DNA. Failing was never an option. Every challenge was a problem to solve, a stepping stone to success. Whenever I questioned my "why," I knew I was doing it for the right reasons – creating a space where culture, community, and personal growth thrived, one sandwich, one story, one connection at a time.

Ultimately, my work ethic got me through each day and looking back it has always been key to achieving what mattered most. Hard work isn't just about perseverance – it's about finding purpose in the process. It taught me tenacity, the ability to push through discomfort, and the satisfaction of knowing I'd given my all. And when work felt easy, it wasn't less valuable – it meant I was working with my gifts, where effort became joy.

Building a business is, at its core, an act of hard work. But the real magic happens when we pair that effort with alignment to our strengths. It's not just about showing up; it's about showing up with intention and purpose, creating something that reflects who we are.

The foundation my parents built through their example has shaped everything I've become. I'll never forget one afternoon during one of my restaurant's busiest lunches. The kitchen was chaotic, tickets piling up, and exhaustion from being there since 1:00 am was settling into my bones. I felt overwhelmed, questioning whether I could keep up with the relentless pace. Then I thought of my father – how he'd awaken before dawn, his hands callused and strong, tackling the day without complaint, always with a quiet pride in his work. I could almost hear his voice, reminding me that "the job isn't done until it's done right." Grounded in that memory, I took a deep breath, rallied my team, and pushed through the day with a renewed sense of purpose. And in that moment, I realized yet again that hard work isn't just about getting through the tough times; it's about how you show up when it matters most.

Success isn't about shortcuts or luck – it's about consistently giving your best, finding fulfillment in the process, and leaning into the joy of doing what matters. Because when we combine effort with purpose, we don't just build businesses; we build lives that are meaningful and impactful.

Sometimes the most important questions we can ask ourselves as entrepreneurs in the thick of our struggles and effort are these: *What is the legacy you're building through the hard work you do every day? Is it just about the tasks you complete, or is it about the impact you're creating, the values you're passing down, and the story you're writing with each effort?*

Hard work isn't just about endurance; it's the catalyst for transformation. It allows you to take an idea, dream, or even simple spark of inspiration and turn it into something tangible – something that lives beyond you. Whether it's a thriving business, a family rooted in strong values, or personal growth that shapes your life's journey, hard work is the force that bridges where you are and where you're meant to be. And in that process, you don't just achieve success, you define it on your own terms.

Letting go isn't failure. It's freedom.
Purpose gives us direction, pride fuels us,
and permission sets us free.

Uztea ez da porrota. Askatasuna da. Helburuak
norabidea ematen digun bezala harrotasunak
bultzada eta baimenak askatzen gaitu.

CHAPTER 9

The Courage to Let Go: The Power of Purpose, Permission, and Pride

As a child, I never really understood the word purpose, but I saw it in motion every single day through my father. He lived with purpose – not in the grandiose, philosophical sense, but in the most tangible way possible. Everything he did was with intention. Whether it was working for someone else, serving customers in the business he built from the ground up, planting his garden, caring for his animals, playing cards, fishing, or simply showing up as someone people could count on, he did it all with quiet but unwavering purpose.

I never heard him give a speech about finding your "why" or your passion like so many do today. But looking back, I realize he didn't have to. His actions were his "why." He embodied it, carrying it in the way he moved through the world – steady, confident, and completely aligned with what mattered to him.

Purpose is more than just knowing why you do something. It's an energy, a force, a fire that propels you forward. It's the deep-seated need to not just exist but to build, create, and contribute in a way that feels meaningful. And with true purpose comes pride – not the ego-driven kind, but the quiet, steady satisfaction. The kind that comes from knowing you've done something well, because it matters and because it is a reflection of who you are.

For as long as I can remember, my father worked with an unstoppable energy. His business was his craft, and his work ethic was unmatched. That's why, when he made the decision to walk away – to sell what he had spent years building – it shocked me. Not because he couldn't, but because I never imagined he would.

But he did. Not because he was forced to. But because he knew his purpose had shifted. He had poured his heart, labor, and soul into building something meaningful, but it was no longer his to nurture. He didn't cling to it. He didn't let his identity stay tied to it. Instead, he gave himself permission to let it go – not with regret, but with peace.

He didn't just sell his business, he released it. He didn't carry the weight of making sure it would be perfect in someone else's hands. He didn't micromanage its future from the sidelines. He had built something great, and now, it was time for the next chapter – one that no longer required him to chase, strive, or prove.

He had nothing to prove. He had built. He had done it. Now, he could just be.

I remember my sister and I worrying that retirement would make him restless, maybe even grow old faster than he had during his whole life – that without work, he would lose the very thing that had always given his life momentum. He had spent his entire life working hard, striving for something better for himself and his family. Surely, stepping away from that drive would leave a void.

But we were wrong. My father thrived just as much in retirement as he did in his working years. Sure, he had a routine. But this time, his life was no longer focused on deadlines, obligations, or responsibilities – it was about living.

His grandkids became his new favorite adventure. Thursdays at my parents' house became legendary – the kids called them "free water park days." When it was irrigation time, he let them run wild in the pasture water, turning a simple farm chore into pure childhood magic. He would laugh as they splashed, completely content just watching them be kids – joyful, free, and full of life.

Fishing trips became another ritual. Of course, he made sure to "help" the grandkids meet their catch limit (or, more accurately, made sure his own fish counted toward theirs). He found joy in every single moment, every simple pleasure.

And, of course, even in retirement, he couldn't sit still.

He found projects to do around the house. He created work just so he'd have more to accomplish. He still took pride in what he did, because that was just who he was.

And sometimes, his determination got the best of him.

Like the day he fell while cleaning up tree trimmings and putting them in the big garbage bin at 79 years old. Instead of immediately seeking help, he finished the job – dragging every last branch to the trash, the trash to the street, and making sure everything was just as it should be. Then, and only then, did he go inside to tell my mother, in his usual calm manner, that he might need to see a doctor.

By the time they got to the hospital, reality set in and he knew he was really hurt. After x-rays and scans, he received the official diagnosis: He had broken his neck.

Two surgeries later, with a will stronger than his body, he tackled his recovery like a man on a mission. Because that's who he was. He didn't sit around, full of self-pity. He didn't dwell on the setback. He got to work healing. Because he had more life to live. More moments to soak in. More memories to create.

I will never forget the look of pure astonishment on his neurosurgeon's face as he watched my father, just shy of 80, heal at a pace that defied logic. It was as if he were witnessing something impossible.

I think, deep down, the doctor doubted he would ever fully recover – let alone regain his strength, independence, and ability to live as though he had never broken his neck at all.

But my father? He never doubted. And just as he always had, he bet on himself and in turn proved the doctor wrong – and his doctor couldn't have been happier.

What my father understood – and what I didn't realize until much later – was that purpose is not fixed. It evolves. It shifts. It grows with us.

The real courage isn't just in pursuing purpose. It's in knowing when to let go. To recognize when a chapter has been completed. To release something that no longer serves us. To trust that there is more ahead, if only we have the courage to move toward it. He gave himself permission to walk away from what no longer served him. And, in turn, he gave me permission too.

The last time I saw my father, I sat across from him, proudly telling him how I had surpassed the seven-figure mark in my business. I had built something incredible. I had worked tirelessly. I was successful.

And he just looked at me and asked:

"But are you happy?"

I opened my mouth to say yes. But before I could even form the words, he stopped me.

"Don't lie to me. I can see it in your eyes."

I was stunned. Because he was right.

I had been unhappy for over a decade – an unhappiness that had little to do with my business and everything to do with who I was and where I was. I didn't fit. I had never truly fit. I had always been drawn to the energy of a city, the hum of life moving all around me, the feeling of both belonging and anonymity at the same time. The kind of place where the chaos matched the firestorm in my mind, where I could lose myself in the rhythm of it all. But I wasn't there - I was somewhere that never felt like mine. And yet, the restaurant became the bridge between where I was and where I longed to be. It was my creation, my attempt at bringing a slice of that energy into a place that didn't hold it naturally. The buzz of the atmosphere, the constant movement, the community – it filled a void I didn't know how else to fill.

Ironically, what gave me a sense of belonging also kept me trapped. The restaurant became my escape. But in the end, it was also my cage. It kept me tethered to a place that could never fully serve me. It gave me purpose, but it also cost me my freedom. The freedom to explore, to visit the places I longed for, to be in the spaces that truly felt like home.

And while I could hide that unhappiness from almost everyone, there was one person who always saw through me. My father. He never pried, never pushed, but he knew. He could see what I had been too afraid to admit.

It was time.

Time to let go of my business – not just physically, but emotionally and mentally. Time to pass the torch and accept that, under someone else's care, it would never be the same. And that was OK. That was the beauty of letting go. It meant trusting that what I had built would grow in new ways beyond me. And for the first time in a long time, I sat really envisioning if that could be enough.

I had done everything I was "supposed" to do. I had built an incredible business that served its community in the best way I knew how. I had created a connection in a town where I had once felt so lost. I tried to show up each day and create an experience that would be better for others and by the standards of success most of us are taught to seek, I had "made it."

I had checked every box:

- Build the business.
- Make the money.
- Prove your worth.

And yet, there I was, exhausted, empty, and stuck, asking myself the same question over and over again:

At what cost? And for whom?

It wasn't just the physical exhaustion of running a restaurant. For years, that part fueled me, it was exhilarating – the challenge, the hustle, the sense of purpose. I had a mission, a place where I belonged. But the real weight, the soul-deep exhaustion, came later, when I had to convince myself it still fit.

My father saw that. And in that last conversation, he gave me something I couldn't give myself: permission.

Permission to step into something new. Permission to pursue the dreams I had put off. Permission to let go, not because what I had built didn't matter, but because its purpose had been served.

He reminded me that what I had created would never be wasted. I had poured my heart and soul into it, and that energy would live on. But it was OK for me to move on. It was OK to find the place that made me happy, that gave me peace.

Deep down, I guess I already knew some of this. I had been thinking about selling my restaurant for some time. I came into this business with an end game plan, but actually making the plan a reality was different. Like my father, I knew my purpose had shifted. I had an opportunity to chase dreams that had been simmering inside me for years, and I also realized that with one of my children off at college and the other leaving the nest soon, I knew this was my chance. But guilt, what others would think, and some self-doubt had been holding me hostage.

I felt bad for wanting to walk away after building this business. The fruits of my labor were finally rewarding me, and now I was ready to set it free? It felt selfish. Unfair.

But my father saw through all of it. He called me out, lovingly but firmly, and gave me the gift I needed most: peace with what I felt in my soul.

He showed me within his words that I didn't need to show up just to "fit in." I was meant to be me. To be OK with just being me. To accept that my purpose had shifted and my impact was made. But mostly he gave me the permission to fully find my happiness and live and do where and what I was meant for – that the courage to take the leap was what mattered most.

I feel like he always reminded me that we only get one shot at this beautiful life, and we have to make it count. And I knew I couldn't waste it living in a way that didn't fulfill me or in a way that would dismiss that my purpose could change.

That conversation with my father was like taking my first real breath in years. In just a few simple words, he did what no one else could – he saw the weight I had been carrying, the exhaustion I had tried to hide, the silent burden that had become so much a part of me I no longer questioned it.

It was crushing me.

The weight of expectations. The weight of holding everything together. The weight of pretending I was OK when I wasn't. And the worst part? I couldn't even put it into words for the people who loved me most. It was a heaviness I had resigned myself to, a burden I thought I had to carry alone.

But he saw it.

And with quiet certainty, he handed me permission to let it go – not just the business, but the suffocating pressure I had wrapped around myself for years. And in that moment, the weight wasn't just lifted. It shattered.

That was the last conversation I ever had with him.

A week later, completely unexpectedly, he was gone.

Grief, no matter how it comes – whether you see it coming or not – is devastating. Losing my father so suddenly was like a punch to the gut, but also a deep slice through my heart. The pain was overwhelming, and the truth I had to face was even harder to bear.

I hadn't spent the kind of time with him that I wanted to. I had convinced myself there would always be more "somedays." But "someday" never came. And the guilt, the loss... it was crushing.

A part of me felt so deeply distraught knowing that I had taken his grandkids out of his daily world when we moved, unintentionally robbing him of the small, everyday moments he cherished most. He never placed that weight on me, never made me feel like I had taken anything from him. But I felt it anyway.

The weight of lost time pressed down on me. The past 10 years replayed in fragments of what-ifs and should-haves, each one a reminder of moments I could never get back. And no matter how much I wished, no matter how many times I turned it over in my mind, I couldn't undo it.

When I walked away after that last conversation with my father, I believed – truly believed – that we would have more time. I thought there would be opportunities to come back, to spend more meaningful moments with my parents, my sister, and everything else I had left behind when we moved. I told myself it was just a matter of "someday" – when the business grew bigger, when the demands of life settled just enough to make getting away or making changes easier.

But life doesn't wait.

And in that moment, faced with the reality of his absence, I was hit with the heartbreaking truth: There was no "someday."

He was gone.

No more hugs. No more conversations. No more chances to make up for the time I had convinced myself I'd eventually have.

He wasn't sick. In fact, he had just received a clean bill of health. He was vibrant, happy, and at peace. How could he be gone? That question haunted me, spinning endlessly in my mind. The disbelief, the ache of loss – it was almost unbearable.

But as I sat with my grief, I found myself reflecting on who my father truly was. The lessons he had lived, often without saying a word. He had always been a man who believed in accepting life's truths, even the ones that didn't make sense. And I realized that, deep down, he had understood something I hadn't yet fully grasped: Our time here is finite. Perhaps it's marked before we ever truly realize the depth and magnitude of our purpose.

He had lived his purpose. And he had passed so much of it on already.

He had long ago given himself permission to let go of what no longer served him. He had chosen to live fully, embracing what brought him joy, staying true to himself, and finding peace in life's transitions. And in that final conversation we shared, he had passed that gift on to me.

In the months that followed his passing, I began preparing myself to let go of my business. It wasn't easy. Letting go never is.

There's the practical side – the endless paperwork, organization, and logistical details. Thankfully, I had kept meticulous records, knowing in the back of my mind that this day would come. But the emotional side? That was far harder.

Selling a business isn't just about passing on a set of keys or leaving behind the business I had built. It was about leaving behind a chapter of my life, closing a door I had held open because it served a deep purpose. It was about honoring the part of me that had created something meaningful while also making room for the next version of myself – the one who was ready to step into something new.

On that last day, as I walked through the doors for the final time, it wasn't the business I grieved. I had already made my peace with letting it go. It was the people. Saying goodbye to the team who had been with me through it all – who had shown up every day with commitment, heart, and drive.

I cried. Not out of regret, but out of gratitude. I hoped they knew how much I appreciated them. How much I valued their role in building something meaningful.

And as I left, I closed the door on one chapter and stepped boldly into the unknown of the next.

At the time, I didn't know what was next. I didn't know that within two years I would be back in business – this time on different terms.

But deep down, I think maybe I did actually always know.

My father's permission and finding my own courage allowed me to take the steps to begin working on creating a new dream. One with freedom, flexibility, and the chance to build something that aligned with all the dreams I hadn't yet pursued.

My father had always understood something so many of us miss: Life is about knowing when it's time to shift. When to embrace something new. When to let go of what no longer serves us.

Letting go isn't failure. It's freedom. Purpose gives us direction, pride fuels us, and permission sets us free.

So when "success" doesn't equal happiness, the real question becomes: *What comes next?*

In business, as in life, we often hold onto things long after their purpose has been fulfilled. Maybe it's a product or service that no longer resonates with our audience but feels too ingrained in our identity to let go. Maybe it's a process, a way of working, or even a mindset that once served us but now keeps us stuck. Or perhaps it's a business itself – something we poured our heart and soul into – that we're afraid to release because we've tied so much of who we are to what we've built.

But the truth is, just as in life, businesses evolve. What once aligned with our purpose might no longer fit. What once brought us joy may now drain us. Growth, both personal and professional, often requires us to take an honest look at what's no longer working – not because it wasn't meaningful, but because its time has passed.

Sometimes, letting go doesn't mean walking away entirely; it might mean breaking things down, refining them, or shifting our focus to make room for what's next. Other times, letting go means releasing the very thing we thought defined us – so that we can discover the freedom, clarity, and alignment waiting on the other side.

Letting go is hard, especially when we've built something with so much pride and effort. But clinging to what no longer serves us out of fear or guilt only holds us back. It keeps us from stepping into the next chapter, the next purpose, the next version of ourselves.

In business, as in life, we must ask ourselves: *Are we holding on because something is still fulfilling us or because we're afraid of what happens when we let go? What if the very thing we're clinging to is keeping us from discovering what's truly meant for us?*

How many of us hold onto things that no longer serve us? A business. A title. An identity. A life we think we're supposed to live because it's what we've built or what we once committed ourselves to. Often, we have attached our identity so tightly to our initial choices and circumstances that we have difficulty even visualising a change. In addition, even those around us possibly don't want to see us change, because that disrupts their ideas of a relationship or how we fit into their lives as well. This all makes the efforts at letting go even harder.

But what if we gave ourselves permission to let go? To shift. To move toward something new. To release what we no longer need, so that we can step fully into what's next.

At the end of the day, no one remembers
the highest balance in your bank account...
They remember the way you helped them
or the way you made them feel.

Egunaren amaieran, inork ez du gogoratzen
zure banku-kontuko saldo handiena...
Gogoratzen dute nola lagundu zenien
edo nola sentiarazi zenien.

CHAPTER 10

Impact: The Wealth That Lasts

My father understood money differently than most. Not as something to chase, not as a status symbol, but as a tool – one that, when managed well, could provide security and freedom. I often wondered whether that perspective came from growing up in a world where money wasn't the currency of success – survival was.

My father grew up in his small village in the Baztan Valley during a time when simply making it through the day was an achievement. He was just a boy when he started crossing the Pyrenees, transporting goods to help his family survive. There was no financial safety net, no backup plan – just the understanding that if he didn't work, there would be no food on the table.

In those years, money wasn't something people had – it was something people traded for value. A sack of flour for a pair of shoes. A day's labor for a meal. Wealth wasn't measured in bank accounts, it was measured in how well you could provide for your family, how much you were willing to work, and how wisely you used what little you had.

That mindset followed him into adulthood and into his business. He never let money define his success, but he respected it. He knew that money – when managed well – meant freedom, stability, choices, and a better life for his children. He didn't pursue wealth, but he also didn't waste it. Every dollar had a purpose, just like every exchange he made as a child in the mountains.

Money is everything and nothing at the same time. It's just a tool, yet it's the tool that opens doors to opportunity, access, and freedom. It won't buy meaning, purpose, or fulfillment, but it shapes the choices to define them. It doesn't define success, but it fuels the ability to potentially create it.

Almost every entrepreneur starts their business with two main goals: making money and gaining freedom – the freedom to control their time, finances, and choices, to build a life on their own terms. They take a skill, passion, or idea and turn it into a business, believing that financial success will bring the independence they've always dreamed of.

And while money is necessary, it's just a tool. A powerful tool, yes, but never the destination. It was never meant to define us and control us or to be the sole measure of success. And yet, for so many business owners, it does and is. They don't just *use* money, they *fear* it. They make decisions from a place of scarcity rather than strategy. And if we're being honest? That kind of relationship with money is exhausting.

When money has power *over* you, no amount ever feels like enough. It will always feel as if you're one bad month away from losing everything. The stress will never ease, the pressure will never lift.

The real shift as a business owner happens when you stop *reacting* to money and start *managing* it. When you see it for what it is – not something to fear, but something you get to *control*. Because when you take ownership of your finances, when you make decisions with clarity rather than fear, you step out of survival mode and into a place of real freedom.

Looking back I realized that, growing up, I learned that money wasn't just something you earned; it was something you managed and controlled. Watching my parents, I saw that financial stability wasn't just about survival, it was about security, freedom, and smart decision-making.

I can still picture my mom at the kitchen table, calculator in hand, methodically managing the books for my father's business. Every cost, every expense accounted for down to the last penny. This same discipline flowed seamlessly into the way she managed our household finances. Every dollar had a purpose.

Even school shopping was part of the budget. My sister and I always had what we needed – not more, not less. It wasn't stingy, it was smart. And without realizing it, my mother had taught us one of the most valuable lessons of all: to appreciate what we had, to make intentional choices, and to understand the difference between want and need.

I'll never forget the first time this lesson really hit home. It was while I was in middle school and Guess jeans were all the rage. Everyone had them and I wanted a pair so badly because I had a real love for fashion. Loving fashion was definitely from my dad – he loved looking at new shoes, clothes, and styles just as much as I did.

When back-to-school shopping rolled around, my mother had a set budget carefully planned, enough for seven new outfits based on typical prices at average stores. But there was one problem: Those Guess jeans I wanted cost more than half the entire budget.

I still remember my mom's calm voice as she laid out the choice: "You can get them if you want, but that means you'll only have two shirts and one pair of jeans for the entire fall wardrobe. The decision is yours."

At that moment, I had to ask myself: *Was it worth it?*

The answer was clear. One pair of jeans wasn't going to get me through the week. I chose seven outfits instead. And just like that, I learned an essential truth for the years to come: We always have the choice to decide how we spend the money we earn. The real question is, what value does it hold for us?

Years later, I realized that business success isn't just about how much money you make, it's about how you view, manage, and direct it. If you're not profiting, the most powerful question you can ask is: *Why? What needs to change?* When you stop fearing money and start managing it with intention, you shift from running your business in panic mode to making decisions with clarity and confidence. The numbers tell a story, revealing what's working, what's not, and where adjustments need to be made. With this awareness, you gain control over your business, making intentional choices to refine, adapt, or pivot when necessary. And that's what ultimately leads you to build the business you envisioned from day one.

Consider the era that existed before money, when humans used the barter system. People traded what they had for what they needed. The exchange was simple: effort for value. My father understood this in a way most people never will.

At just 10 years old, he began crossing the Pyrenees Mountains, transporting goods during war and hardship. People didn't have luxurious wealth; they had survival. Sometimes, the exchange was made with money, but more often, it was goods for goods, labor for resources, skill for necessity.

And that principle still applies to business today: Money flows where value is created.

So many entrepreneurs believe that if they just make more money, everything will fall into place. That more revenue will somehow fix the stress, the uncertainty, the feeling of never quite having enough. But the truth is, many don't even know where their money is going. They avoid their numbers out of fear, undercharge out of insecurity, or overprice out of desperation. They overwork themselves without a clear strategy, stuck in a cycle of burnout, constantly seeking more, yet never feeling in control.

More money isn't always the answer. The real challenge isn't the amount, it's the fear. Fear of facing the numbers, fear of managing finances, fear of what you might uncover. It's not a lack of income that keeps entrepreneurs stuck; it's avoidance and a lack of control over their money that creates the real struggle.

Now imagine this instead: At the end of each month, you know exactly where your revenue went because you assigned every dollar a purpose. You're no longer making decisions from a place of panic, but from a place of strategy. Instead of wondering whether you can afford to invest in your business, you've already planned for it.

Money isn't a runaway train. It's a vehicle, and you are in the driver's seat. You are not at the mercy of your bank balance. If you are willing to work for money, to exchange your energy to earn it, then you also have the *right* to control it. Where your money flows, how it's used, and what it builds – it's all in your hands.

Many years ago, in my early days of entrepreneurship, I unknowingly abandoned the financial principles I had grown up with. Instead of managing money with intention, I let it control me. Fear – fear of not having enough, fear of failure, fear of making the wrong move – dictated my every decision. I stressed over every dollar, making scarcity-driven financial choices without truly understanding the numbers or the mindset from which I was operating.

I fell into the trap of believing that doing everything myself would save money. I took on tasks the hardest way possible, spending countless hours on work that drained me – work that, in hindsight, stole precious time I could have invested in tasks that actually moved my business forward. I was stuck in a relentless cycle of stress and anxiety, feeling like I was always one step away from losing everything. Money wasn't a tool I controlled; it was a weight pressing down on me, keeping me up at night, stealing my presence from the moments that mattered.

It was exhausting. Utterly depleting.

But through that rollercoaster of uncertainty, and with some much-needed reminders from my upbringing, I worked hard to shift my mindset and redefine my relationship with money. I learned to see it as a resource to be managed, not as a threat to be feared. I let go of the belief that more effort always meant more success and started making decisions based on strategy, not scarcity.

Two businesses and many years later, that shift I learned early in my entrepreneurial years shaped the way I built my restaurant. It changed the way I approached profit, efficiency, and growth. And I truly believe it played a major role in reaching my financial goals.

I became so in tune with numbers that profitability became less of a pressure point and more of a challenge – not in a ruthless, cutthroat way, but in a way that pushed me to think differently. I treated it like a game of strategy, problem-solving, and impact, constantly looking for ways to maximize efficiency, drive profits, and run a thriving business without sacrificing quality or customer experience.

For me, success was never about cutting corners or stripping away value just to save a few dollars. The sacrifice was never quality. It was never customer service. Instead, I leaned into curiosity. No day was ever perfect, but every day was an opportunity to learn, to ask better questions, to refine, and to adapt. Every decision was driven by the same goal: to make the business stronger, more profitable, and more impactful.

My mindset shifted from fearing the numbers to studying them. I started asking the right questions:

- *Why did those expenses go up?*
- *Why did the bottom line change?*
- *How can we adjust and make it better?*
- *How can we refine our systems to make service smoother?*
- *How can we maximize every dollar without sacrificing quality?*
- *How can we create an unforgettable customer experience – not because we're the cheapest, but because people love our product and trust us?*

In the end, the solution was never about just cutting costs, it was about creating more value. Keeping the business lean, efficient, and impactful led to something incredible; profits didn't just stabilize, they grew. And as they did, I realized something profound: I had come full circle.

I had returned to the very lesson my parents instilled in me – that money is a tool to be managed, not feared. And when used wisely, it doesn't just build a profitable business, it builds a meaningful one.

That principle still guides me in business today. Profit isn't the only goal, it's the result of intentional decisions, smart money management, and most importantly, the impact we create.

Profit is the byproduct of impact made and money managed well. When you build a business that solves real problems, when you lead with purpose, when you focus on delivering value, the money naturally follows.

Let me give you an example. Imagine two restaurants:

- Restaurant A: Obsessed with making money. They cut corners, sacrifice quality, and charge as much as possible while giving as little as they can. They're constantly stressed, looking for customers, offering endless discounts, or wondering where everyone is.

- Restaurant B: Focused on the experience. They serve food with heart, make people feel welcome, and build relationships. They're still strategic with pricing, but profit is a byproduct of their excellent service and product, not their sole focus. And because they prioritize impact, value, and consistency, customers return. They tell their friends. They don't need to run after money or customers, because money finds them.

This applies to every business. A marketing strategist

who only chases sales might get clients but will struggle to keep them. A coach who builds trust and delivers real results doesn't have to sell so hard; clients will materialize through word-of-mouth reviews and stay for the long haul. A product business that focuses solely on quick transactions will wonder where all its customers went. But a product business that solves a real need, builds a strong brand, and serves its customers like they matter will be profitable for years.

Growing up, I was taught to respect money – not as the measure of success, but as something to manage with care, ensuring freedom, stability, and security. My father never tied his business success to the amount of money he made. I often wonder if that perspective came from the life he lived in his youth – the kind of life where simply making it through the day was an achievement. Where survival wasn't guaranteed, and money – if it was there at all – wasn't something you could rely on.

For him, success wasn't about hitting a number in the bank account. It was about showing up, putting in an honest day's work, and doing right by the people who depended on him. It was about coming home after a long day, sitting around the dinner table with his family, and knowing he had provided -not just financially, but also in terms of presence, love, and the way he made us feel safe.

I watched my father build his business not by trailing after money, but by earning trust. He understood that money could come and go, sometimes in an instant. But character, reputation, integrity – those were the things that lasted. That belief shaped everything about how he lived and led. Maybe that's why he never chased money for its own sake. Perhaps deep down he knew the real legacy for him would never be found in a bank account. It was found in how you showed up, how you treated others, and how you stayed true to who you were, even when no one was watching.

Every decision he made came back to three simple things:

- Who he could help;
- The work he could be proud of;
- The impact he could make.

Money mattered, of course. But it was never the driving force. He didn't serve his community to make money; he made money because he served his community. And he did it with integrity.

He could have taken shortcuts. He could have saved time by skipping the small finishing touches, by not edging every time he mowed a lawn, knowing most customers wouldn't notice. He could have installed cheaper sprinkler systems that would fail sooner, keeping customers coming back for repairs.

But that wasn't how he did business.

Instead, he played the long game. He used quality materials, even when it meant making less in the short term. He installed sprinklers that lasted, not ones that guaranteed him repeat work. He edged every lawn, every single time, even when no one was watching. Because he would know. He took pride in the details, in the quality of his work, in doing things the right way.

And the impact? It came full circle.

Customers stayed. They trusted him. They told their friends. His reputation spread, not because of flashy marketing or low prices, but because of the way he made people feel valued, cared for, and respected. That was his success. That was his wealth. And that was the lesson he left behind.

When you build a business with integrity, when you focus on impact over quick profits, when you take pride in what you do, the money will always follow.

His customers stayed. They trusted him. And most importantly, they told people. Three, five, 10 more customers would hear about how a customer's irrigation system never failed, how their yard was always done right, how their gardener was different, someone who actually cared.

That lesson I learned from him stuck with me through life.

Years later, when I owned my restaurant, I found myself thinking about him often. Thinking about what he would have done if he were in the same position. Food costs were always fluctuating, and in the restaurant industry, there was constant talk about ways to cut costs. The talk revolved around finding cheaper ingredients, swapping for lower-quality products, reducing portions to stretch margins. It was tempting, especially when I watched competitors take those shortcuts and temporarily increase their profit margins.

But every time, I thought of my father and his sprinkler systems.

If I wouldn't eat it, why would I serve it? If I wouldn't be proud of it, why would I sell it?

The answer was simple: I wouldn't.

Just like my father, I chose the long game. I refused to cut corners on quality, even when it meant a smaller margin that month. And just like him, I saw the impact come full circle. Customers came back. They trusted us. They told their friends. We built a foundation of quality, integrity, and trust. Not on squeezing out a few extra dollars at the expense of what truly matters.

Short-term profits will never outweigh long-term reputation. And my father understood that better than anyone. He never measured success by the money he made but by the impact he left behind. For him, money was never the goal; it was simply the byproduct of doing good work, serving people well, and building something that mattered.

When money is the only measure of success, no amount will ever feel like enough. The chase never stops, the pressure never lifts, and the fear of losing it never goes away. But when you lead with impact – when you focus on creating real value, solving real problems, and serving people in a way that matters – fulfillment comes first, and income follows naturally.

It's a cycle: Impact attracts business → business generates income → income fuels more impact. And when that income is managed wisely, you don't just create wealth, you build something sustainable for the long term.

When you prioritize impact:

- Customers come to you – you don't have to pursue them.
- You don't have to discount to compete; people pay full price happily.
- Your team thrives because they believe in your vision and purpose.

The entrepreneur who builds with intention, who leads with service, and who focuses on providing value will always have money flowing in because people invest in things that change their lives.

The chef who pours their heart into every dish. The coach who delivers real strategies that have created lasting results. The business owner who genuinely cares about their customers. When you lead your business with purpose, profit always follows.

This same philosophy of impact translates into giving. Have you ever noticed how some of the most successful business owners freely give, whether it's knowledge, time, products, content, or resources? Generosity is a magnet for abundance.

I've seen it, experienced it, and lived it. The business owner who shared valuable insights with their audience for free ended up with a loyal customer base that trusted them enough to buy everything they offered. The restaurant owner that donated free meals to students built a reputation that led to those students becoming lifelong customers, fueling long-term growth. The entrepreneurs who freely shared their skills and tools to help other business owners succeed found doors opening to opportunities they had never imagined.

Money flows where value is created. Often the more value you give, the more you receive – not as a simple transaction, but as the ripple effect of true impact and giving with joy.

At the end of the day, no one remembers the highest balance in your bank account. No one talks about what your business profited in Q4 five years ago. But they do remember the way you helped them or the way you made them feel.

They remember the way your business solved a problem, made their lives easier, helped them grow, or simply gave them something worth believing in.

Money alone doesn't create joy. But knowing your work changes lives? That's a kind of success that no amount of money can replace.

There's a misconception that business success is purely about making money. But time and time again, I've seen the opposite to be true.

The most fulfilled and successful business owners, the ones who not only make money but truly love what they do, aren't on the hunt for dollars. Money alone won't bring fulfillment. We all know plenty of financially wealthy people who are miserable. And chasing money alone doesn't always bring more money. In fact, it often causes business owners to miss the key factors that create lasting success. The most fulfilled entrepreneurs realize that money will always follow impact, and that fulfillment will always bring true prosperity.

Perhaps the richest kind of wealth is the kind where you take your purpose, create real impact, and in turn build a profitable business. True wealth isn't just financial; it's the ability to make a difference while still enjoying financial freedom.

If you really think about it, your life legacy is built on impact. Ultimately, people remember how you made them feel, not what you earned. Wealth isn't just what's in your bank account; it's the currency of your relationships, reputation, and personal fulfillment.

At my father's funeral, a doctor – one of his longtime customers – walked up to me. His eyes carried both grief and gratitude as he introduced himself. Then, with a soft smile, he told me something I wasn't expecting.

"For years, your father was a regular topic at our family dinners," he shared. "Even now, long after my kids have grown up and moved out, they still talk about him."

His kids used to love the days my father arrived with his crew. The moment they heard his truck pull up, they would grab their little toy lawnmowers and rush outside, eager to "help" in their own way. My father always took a moment to acknowledge them – to ask about their latest toy, listen to their excited chatter, or just share a warm hello – before getting to work. It was a small thing, but it mattered.

For almost 30 years, my father wasn't just their gardener. He was part of their lives. He and his crew showed up every week, rain or shine, with the same unwavering warmth and kindness. He never cut corners, never rushed through his work just to get to the next job. He took pride in what he did, and because of that, he built something most business owners grasp at for their entire lives – loyalty, trust, and a reputation that lasted beyond his years.

His customers valued him not just for his work, but for who he was. That's the power of impact in business.

I often think about how, despite having only a third-grade education, my father built something that many highly educated, well-off customers deeply respected. He had customers who had advanced degrees, ran successful companies, and had financial wealth beyond anything he had ever known. Yet, they admired *him* – not because of his net worth, but because of the integrity he brought to his work, the relationships he built, and the way he made them feel.

My father often spoke about his lack of education as if it were his greatest weakness. He never said it outright, but we could sense it – the quiet wish that he would have been given the chance to learn beyond the third grade. For a man who questioned everything and had an insatiable drive to understand the world, it was no surprise.

But if there was one thing he was certain of, it was that my sister and I *would* go to college. There was never a question, only a promise. He believed education was the key to the opportunities he never had, and he was determined to help us open doors that had always remained closed to him. No matter what it took, he would find a way to support us, because to him, knowledge meant possibility.

What's ironic is that while he saw education as a missing piece, his life's work proved that intelligence isn't confined to a classroom. My father was one of the smartest and most emotionally intuitive people I've ever known. Understanding people was his superpower. His problem-solving skills were unmatched, his curiosity made him unstoppable, and his ability to adapt was second nature. He never dwelled on what he *didn't* have; instead, he focused on what he *could* do. And with that mindset, he poured his energy into building a business that truly mattered.

My father never worried about competition. He never had to pursue customers. They came to him. They stayed with him. They paid him well. Because he built his business on service, relationships, and showing up fully, and what an incredible business he built.

That's what happens when you run a business with excellence, care, and integrity. When you create an experience people can't forget.

Money and making a profit in business is imperative. We have to make a profit or we don't get to stay in business. Money gives us choices, freedom, and the ability to live a comfortable life. But what if we chose to see money differently?

What if, instead of seeing money and purpose as separate conversations, we embraced them as partners? What if we stopped treating profit and impact as opposing forces and recognized that the most successful businesses do both?

Impact isn't just a feel-good concept. It's a powerful strategy for long-term success. Yet, so many business owners fall into the trap of survival mode, convinced that making more money will fix everything. But without a clear purpose and direction, money slips through the cracks. And a business that lacks impact doesn't just struggle; it stagnates, unable to grow sustainably or build lasting success.

So, what if instead of chasing money, you built your business with the certainty that there will always be enough, because you're creating real value that people are willing to pay for? What if you took control of your money instead of letting it control you?

Are you building a business just to make money, or are you creating something bigger than yourself? If money was no longer the scoreboard for success, what would success actually mean to you?

Everything starts with intention. Profit without purpose is empty, and purpose without profit isn't sustainable. The most powerful businesses, the ones that thrive, fulfill, and leave a legacy, are built where purpose fuels impact, impact fuels profit, and profit is intentionally directed to create even greater wealth and impact.

Legacy is shaped in the quiet moments —
in the way we show up when no one is watching.

Ondarea une isiletan moldatzen da — inork begira ez
dugunean azaltzen garen moduan.

CHAPTER 11

The Legacy We Build and Leave Behind

From a young age, I've been captivated by the idea of legacy. Even as a teenager, I often found myself reflecting on a single, compelling question: *What will I leave behind? How will I be remembered when my story fades into whispered conversations or becomes part of a final farewell?* It might sound morbid to some but, to me, it's a beautifully inspiring reminder. We each have the power to shape how we live this one extraordinary life and determine the mark we'll leave on the world long after we're gone.

Legacy, at its simplest, is something passed on. Yet it is so much more profound, complex, and meaningful than just inheritance or possessions. Legacy encompasses the values we embody, the principles we uphold, and the genuine impact we leave in the hearts of those around us. It can be financial and tangible, certainly, but more profoundly, it is emotional, spiritual, and personal. Legacy lives in the memories we create, the lessons we teach, and the way we make people feel.

Most of us navigate life pursuing success, happiness, or purpose often without realizing we're simultaneously building our legacy. Whether we acknowledge it or not, our daily actions, decisions, and interactions weave together the picture we will someday leave behind. It is not just a collection of grand accomplishments but rather the countless smaller moments, how we respond to adversity, the kindness we offer without expectation, the integrity we show when nobody is watching.

As I've grown older, my understanding of legacy has deepened and expanded. I've realized that the most meaningful aspects of our legacy cannot be bought or measured; they exist in the intangible gifts we pass down, the values we instill, and the examples we set by simply living authentically. But what I also realize is that I was lucky enough to have a real example of what this looks like modeled in front of me my whole life.

My father's impact has always been a guiding light for me, shaping both my personal beliefs and professional values. His life taught me that real success isn't measured solely by accomplishments or status, but largely by being a good human and by serving and respecting ourselves and those we serve and find community among. His life was the clearest example of this truth. His legacy was not defined merely by his achievements in business or the possessions he acquired, but by the way he chose to live every single day.

Through his warmth, resilience, steadfast support, and humor, he created countless meaningful moments, intentionally and unintentionally shaping the lives around him. I'm not even sure he actually knew the impact he had on those around him, but as we witnessed at his memorial and during the many months after, it was profound.

Through the words spoken by his brothers, sisters, friends, customers, and generations of immediate and extended family, it became strikingly clear: His true legacy wasn't measured by accomplishments or accolades. It lived in the laughter he inspired, the wisdom he quietly shared, and his infectious love for life and its endless possibilities.

But the beauty of legacy is that it rarely announces itself in grand gestures.

It's found in the small, consistent acts and everyday choices – the way we show up for people, the energy we bring into a room. That's where legacy takes root. And nowhere was that more evident, especially during his memorial and the months that followed, than in the eyes of the youngest generation as they talked about their "Aitatxi" (grandfather in Basque).

They shared stories one by one. It began with my nephew recognizing him as a protector, provider, and survivor. He described his grandfather as someone who safeguarded our family and preserved our way of life through his teachings. His work ethic and vast knowledge were his way of providing. Coming from a time when food was scarce, Aitatxi didn't just talk about survival – he *lived* it. Every animal, plant, or tree in his yard had a purpose. If it was growing, it was feeding. If it was alive, it had value.

To him, nothing existed "just because." That wasn't how he thought, and it wasn't how he raised us. He taught us, without ever preaching, that everything in life has a place and a purpose. That belief showed up in the way he moved through the world – in the way he fixed things, built things, and took care of what was important.

But purpose didn't mean life was all seriousness. In fact, some of Aitatxi's most lasting lessons came wrapped in laughter and surprise. He had a way of turning even the simplest outing into an unexpected adventure – and sometimes those adventures came with wild twists you could never see coming.

As the stories flowed, my niece recalled one of her favorite memories at Galena Pond, their go-to fishing spot. When they arrived one day, they found a busload of school kids had taken over the shoreline. Aitatxi wasn't thrilled – he figured the noise would scare the fish. But after an hour of no bites and a lot of kid-sized commotion down the bank, he leaned over and said, "Go find out what they're using."

Turns out, the kids' secret weapon was sweet corn. "We switched bait, and *bam* – instant success," she said. But that wasn't even the wildest part.

As she cast her line again, something felt off – too heavy, too soon. She reeled it in, and to their shock, she had accidentally hooked a chipmunk. "A chipmunk!" she underscored the absurdity. "That little guy must've been trying to snag a bite of corn and ended up airborne. We laughed hysterically. Aitatxi gently removed it from the hook, wrapped it carefully in a plastic grocery bag, and to my surprise, decided to take it home. Everyone loved it – except my grandma, who insisted the chipmunk be returned to the pond immediately due to health concerns."

Looking back, my niece said that day wasn't just about fishing. It was a snapshot of who he was – curious, adaptable, funny, a little mischievous, and always thinking 10 steps ahead. He taught her that sometimes the best stories are the ones you never plan for.

And while adventure seemed to follow him everywhere, what made those moments unforgettable was the joy he infused into all of it. It wasn't just what we did together – it was how he made it *feel*. Joy, I've come to realize, was one of the greatest legacies he left us.

All four grandkids lit up as they segued into the next story, laughing and smiling as they remembered their favorite day of the week growing up. Thursdays were irrigation days, but for the grandkids, they were transformed into private waterpark days. The backyard became their playground, and Aitatxi never stopped them from getting messy or wild.

Our fishing trips became mini adventures. He had a rule: If a fish wasn't up to his standard, it got thrown back. "We'll catch a bigger one," he'd say.

Then my daughter took us down memory lane to her 4H days. Her lamb, Josie, ended up... well, a little rounder than she should've been at weigh-in. Turns out, Aitatxi had been sneaking Josie extra scoops of grain behind her back, just to make sure she was never hungry. He thought he was helping – and in a way, he was. It was his love language. Always feeding. Always giving.

She also brought up the good memories they made in the treehouse. She remembered how Aitatxi would fix it with his signature Basque ingenuity – using whatever scraps he had on hand to make something strong and functional. It may not have passed a safety inspection, but it was ours. And it was magic.

They all said it countless times: There was never a dull moment. And looking back now, they were right. He found magic in the ordinary – and then taught all of his grandkids to do the same.

But his legacy wasn't just built in moments of laughter and play. It was also rooted in the quiet, unwavering presence he gave us, the kind of love that didn't need words to be felt.

He wasn't always vocal, but his pride in his family ran deep. He showed up to every sporting event he could, cheering with that big, proud smile of his. He didn't say much, but you *knew* how much he loved you.

That was his way. Strong. Steady. Always there.

And as they laughed and remembered the stories they'd been sharing, my son – the youngest grandchild – added a few more of his own. "Aitatxi taught us how to work hard, how to eat well, and how to play Mus," the Basque card game that's all about strategy, bluffing, memory, and maybe a little luck. "And he wasn't just good – he was a US champion. He even won a trip to Argentina to compete in the world tournament."

But what I remember most wasn't his title. It was sitting across from him at the kitchen table, learning how to think five steps ahead, and laughing every time he caught me trying to bluff.

Aitatxi made the ordinary feel extraordinary. Even errands turned into adventures. We'd go to the local nurseries, Total Wine, Sportsman's Warehouse, even Walmart, just to see what was new. He was never bored, and he refused to be bored. He lived with a kind of energy that said, "Life is too short not to enjoy every second."

That energy, that presence, that joyful pursuit of life – that was his legacy. Not because he tried to leave one, but because he simply lived fully, loved deeply, and showed up with intention.

And that's when it really hit me: Legacy isn't some far-off thing we only think about at the end of life. It's something we create every single day – whether we realize it or not.

Legacy doesn't always come from words. Sometimes, it comes from showing up, again and again. From fixing the thing that broke. From never missing a game. From being the person your grandkids want to spend every Thursday with.

And sometimes, legacy is built in the comfort of the familiar – the rhythms of daily life, the small rituals that leave a lasting imprint. Even the simplest days with him left a lasting impression rich with meaning, filled with laughter, lessons, and love that quietly took root.

What truly brought it all home for me was witnessing how legacy weaves itself not just through generations, but within them, shaping how they see the world, how they move through it, and how they carry the spirit of someone long after they've gone.

I saw just how deeply he had impacted all of our lives, not through lectures or grand gestures, but in the way he lived, laughed, and loved. The everyday moments, ones filled with curiosity, care, and just the right amount of mischief. Through their eyes, I saw not just who he was, but the joyful, grounded, generous energy he passed on without even trying.

He never set out to create a legacy. That wasn't his intention. But maybe that's exactly what makes it so powerful. Legacy isn't something we announce or strive to manufacture – it's something we build, quietly and consistently, in the everyday ways we choose to show up, especially when no one's looking.

And for my father, that showed up most clearly in the way he lived with purpose. Not just in the big, obvious ways, but in every detail, every action, every choice. His legacy was rooted in how he provided, how he protected, and how he ensured that nothing – absolutely nothing – was wasted or without meaning.

These stories told through those hard days illustrate the profound truth I've come to understand – that each moment we live, every decision we make, and every interaction we have contributes to the legacy we get to leave behind. Legacy isn't something we wait until the end of life to think about. It's built now. It's built in how we show up, how we treat people, what we believe in, and what we pass on – through laughter, through love, through living life fully.

And this doesn't just apply to our families or our personal lives. It carries into the businesses we build. Every client interaction, every decision made with integrity, every moment we lead with curiosity and heart – it all matters. It all adds up. Whether in life or in business, we create legacy daily through our actions, our values, and the genuine connections we build.

And maybe the most powerful legacy of all is the one we didn't even know we were leaving behind – the kind remembered in the hearts of our grandchildren or the youngest generation of lives, retold with laughter, love, and the glint of a chipmunk-sized memory.

Legacy in Business: The Path We Create Through How We Build

Legacy isn't limited to family trees or generational storytelling. It stretches into the work we do, the businesses we build, and the impact we leave long after we've stepped away.

Because when you think about it, a business is so much more than a brand, a product, or a profit margin. It's a living, breathing reflection of who we are, our values, our vision, our quirks, our decisions. It's an echo of how we choose to show up in the world.

We often think of a business as a job or what we do, something that demands our time and energy. But what if we flipped the lens? What if, instead, we asked ourselves: *What legacy am I building through this business? What do I want my clients, my team, my community, even my family to remember about how I led, how I served, and how I showed up?*

When I think about my father – how he made his customers and families feel seen by just taking a few minutes to have a conversation, turned irrigation days into water parks for his grandkids, or made a trip to Walmart feel like an adventure – it reminds me that business, too, can be infused with joy, personality, and purpose. That we get to decide how it feels to work with us. We get to create cultures where people feel seen. We get to design systems that honor freedom. We get to build in ways that align with who we are, not just what the industry says we should be.

And that's a legacy worth building.

But this idea of legacy goes even deeper. It's not just about the people who know us now. It's about the invisible ripple effect of how we show up, day after day, and how that *builds something real*, even if we don't see it right away.

A business isn't separate from life. It's a circle within the greater circle of who we are and how we live. It holds our stories. Our resilience. Our vision. It holds the hard days and the breakthroughs. The lessons we've learned, and the wisdom we offer through every product, every service, every solution.

Most people see their business as something they *do*, but what if we saw it as something we're *becoming through*? I always marvel at how incredible it is that the transformation we make as entrepreneurs is who we become as people. I truly believe so much of this transformation is because our business is a sacred extension of our lives. A container for our creativity, generosity, values, and unique way of showing up and serving people while also being so fulfilled too. Our business and who we are represent a mutually beneficial relationship. It's an exchange, an evolution, a living partnership that shapes us as much as we shape it.

Yes, it pays the bills, but it also carries our fingerprints in a thousand unseen ways.

When I sold my first business, I knew from the beginning it was only a stepping stone, part of a bigger vision I hadn't fully shaped yet. I built it with intention, knowing it wasn't my forever path. And yet, I never could've predicted how deeply that first experience would leave its mark on me, or how much it would teach me about the quiet power of legacy.

Even now, years later, that brand still exists. The name. The signage. The identity. It's evolved, of course – reshaped by time and new leadership – but pieces of what we created still live on. That in itself is a kind of legacy.

Fast forward to the restaurant and catering business, and legacy showed up again, but in a deeper, more personal way. Letting go of that business wasn't easy. I knew I had served my purpose, and that it was time to move on. But walking away from something you've poured your soul into is never clean-cut. You hope what you built remains recognizable, that the culture you nurtured stays intact. But once it's no longer yours, it's no longer yours.

And that's part of the deal: When you sell, you don't get to choose how the new owner carries the legacy forward. You only get to choose how you let go.

The truth is, we all do business differently. We bring our own values, our own rhythm, our own way of doing things. But what's so beautiful about legacy in business is this:

Long after the sale is finalized, long after the keys are handed over, people will remember the way you made them *feel*. Not just the product. But the presence. The care. The integrity.

That's the kind of legacy I continue to hold close.

It's what led me to this next chapter of my life – and the beginning of **Bideako** which in the Basque language means "on the path" or "pathways." In this case, it means Pathways to business success.

I'll never forget the first year of building Bideako as a business educator and mentor. I started it because I love teaching. I love sharing information. I love sharing ideas and I seem to have a million of them buzzing in my brain. I love small businesses. I love helping people reach a potential they couldn't yet see in themselves. But more than anything, I love watching people come back to life – watching them realize that business could be a path back to themselves.

One of my earliest clients came to me completely overwhelmed, stuck in a cycle of decision fatigue. She was constantly second-guessing her direction, unsure how to make her business feel like something more than just survival. I still remember the way she looked at me and said, "I just want to feel like I'm building something that brings me joy – not something that's eating me alive." That moment hit hard, because I've been there too. We all get caught in the grind. We pursue someone else's version of success, follow the blueprints, check the boxes, do what we think we're "supposed" to do. But somewhere in all that noise, we forget the most important thing: *The way you build your business becomes part of your legacy.*

It's not just about the numbers; it's about the energy behind them. It's not just about the systems; it's about what those systems make possible in your *actual* life. It's not just about the end result; it's about who you're becoming along the way.

That realization took root in me years earlier, when I was running the restaurant and catering business. At that time, I found myself constantly asking: *Does this align with my life? With my values? With what truly matters to me?* For me, that meant my children and family came first. They were the priority, and everything else had to align around that. It influenced the way I structured the business, the kind of work I took on, and even how I defined success. I didn't want to build something that looked perfect on paper but left me feeling disconnected from the people I loved most. I wanted success that didn't come at the cost of presence, a life where I could grow something meaningful and still nurture relationships with my kids. That kind of inner alignment became my compass.

Then and now, I'm reminded of a simple truth which I see play out every single day in business: Legacy doesn't have to be loud or elaborate.

If we pause long enough to really notice what's taking shape, we realize that legacy is most often built quietly. In the way you take time to answer an email with care. In the way you choose truth over ego. In the way you keep showing up with integrity, even when no one's watching.

What I've come to understand from watching my father and learning about so many incredible business stories, the most beautiful part is this: Your legacy often builds itself when you're not even trying to build it. You just stay aligned. You lead with heart. You serve with intention.

And in doing so, you leave behind something unforgettable. Not because you planned a legacy, but because you *lived* it.

So maybe the question isn't just: *What are you building?* Maybe it's also: *How are you building it? Who are you becoming in the process? What invisible thread are you weaving into the lives of others just by doing your work with purpose, intention, and love?*

That's what makes this all worth it. That's the business within the greater circle of life. And that's a legacy no one can ever take away.

The path forward isn't about doing more. It's about doing more of what matters.

Aurrera egiteko bidea ez da gehiago egitea, baizik eta garrantzitsuena dena gehiago egitea

The Business of Becoming

This book began as a tribute – not just to my father's journey, but to the path I've walked because of him. His story shaped every part of who I've become – not only as a first-generation American, but as someone navigating two cultures, raising a family, building businesses, and now mentoring others as they find success on their own terms.

The year before I began writing this book, everything in my world was shifting. I had sold the restaurant. My husband retired from his 30 year career in education. Our kids were grown and gone, and the house was quiet in a way that didn't feel peaceful – it felt hollow. I was living in a place that didn't feed my soul, carrying a kind of loneliness that settled deep. I was in my mid-40s, staring down a new chapter I knew I was ready for, but had no idea how to begin. My father was no longer with us. The one who always saw me clearly, who knew when to push and when to soften, had gone quiet. His chair sat empty, but his presence never left. And in that silence, I found myself searching – not just for him, but for the parts of me that only he ever fully understood.

In the midst of gathering ideas, forming my thoughts, and wondering if I truly had a book in me, I returned to the Basque Country with my husband – not just as a daughter, but as a woman on a mission to see my roots through new eyes. I visited the mountains my father once crossed as a boy – the same border between Spain and France he walked at just 10 years old, carrying a sack heavier than he was and a dream even bigger. I stood in the caves once whispered about in folklore, where healing was drawn from the land itself. And I felt something awaken in me – a quiet reminder of resilience, curiosity, intuition, and the power of where we come from.

I reconnected with family – cousins, aunts, uncles I'd only known in moments we vacationed, short visits, and memories – and despite the years and distance, I felt a kind of home. As if a part of me had been waiting for this kind of comfort. I enrolled in an immersive Basque language class and relearned the language I'd grown up around. And somehow, through the words, it felt like my father was speaking to me again.

Writing this book gave me peace with dreams I had once put down. It reminded me how far I've come, and how much is still ahead. It showed me that the chapters I thought were finished were simply waiting for me to return with a new perspective.

And during those months of writing, something else became clear: Bideako wasn't just a new business. It was the work I'd been preparing for all along. A place where I get to walk alongside other entrepreneurs – those building something meaningful, not just for profit, but for purpose. People who are becoming through their business journey, just like I did.

Teaching, guiding, mentoring, encouraging – this is what lights me up. But beyond the strategies, beyond the growth and the systems, what I hope people feel when they work with me is knowing that they matter and they absolutely can build a business that fulfills them and a life that they love.

Because that's what I learned from my father, from my family, and from the many stories left behind. Legacy isn't built on accolades. It's built on how we make people feel. How we show up. How we serve others in fulfilling our own purpose. What we choose to preserve.

Our lives, and the businesses we pour ourselves into, are shaped by the choices we make every single day. Not just the big ones. The quiet ones too. The ones no one sees but us.

Success? It's never been about just having a dream or working hard. It's about making intentional choices that feel aligned with who we are, what we value, and how we want to show up in this world. It's about persistence, resilience, and learning to keep going; not because it's easy, but because it matters.

And if I've learned anything through all of this, it's this: Our greatest power is our ability to choose.

When I sat down to write this final chapter, I knew I wasn't here to wrap everything up in a tidy little bow. Life doesn't work that way. And if you've ever run a business, you know that's not how it goes either. It's messy. It's nonlinear. It's beautiful. What I wanted to leave you with wasn't a checklist, it was a perspective. Something real. Something human.

At its core, this story isn't just about life or business. It's about becoming. We search for freedom, flexibility, and impact, but the real gift is who we become along the way.

And the truth? Success was never just about the hustle. It's about making choices – quiet, intentional ones – that reflect who we are and what we value. It's about showing up even when it's hard. Especially when it's hard.

My father's legacy lives in me. His grit, humility, curiosity, faith… they've shaped every chapter. Each lesson I've shared is a thread in that story:

- Curiosity kept me open. Every breakthrough began with a question.
- Clarity helped me block out the noise and move with purpose.
- Letting go taught me trust and the quiet power of surrender.
- Hard work was never the problem; it was knowing where to focus.
- Purpose gave meaning to it all.
- And legacy? It's not built in loud moments. It's shaped in how we treat people. How we lead. How we live.

Sometimes we have to unlearn what no longer serves us. We have to trust blurry visions, get scrappy, stumble forward, and find wins in the places we least expect. And through it all, we keep showing up, because when something matters, that's exactly what we do.

I still believe we're building legacy in real time. And maybe we always have been.

A beautiful and wise centenarian once told me the secret to a joyful life: Find peace within yourself. And maybe, just maybe, that's what we're all really looking for – not just in life, but in business, too.

So I'll leave you with a few questions, ones I ask myself:

- What do I want my business to make possible – for my life, my family, and those I serve?

- Where am I still playing small?

- What would it look like to lead with intention, not obligation?

- If my business became my legacy, what would I want it to say?

You don't need all the answers. Just the next step that feels aligned – aligned with who you are, what you value, and the kind of life and business you're here to build. Alignment isn't just what makes sense on paper, it's what feels right in your gut, steady in your bones. It's the step that reflects your truth, honors your voice, and moves you closer to a life that feels fully your own. It's the choice that feels like you, even if it's scary, especially if it sets you free.

The path forward isn't about doing more. It's about doing more of what matters. Building something real. With impact, not just impressions. With alignment, not just approval.

And showing up fully – not just for your business, but for your life.

The finish line? That's yours to define.

But the turning points, the deep breaths, the bold leaps? Those are what shape our path.

My dad always believed this life wasn't something to conquer, but something to cherish. It's a one-time journey meant to be felt, not just figured out. And when we live from that place, we realize we already have so much more than we think we have.

So wherever you are right now... let this be your moment.

Let your heart stay open, your wonder stay wild, and don't forget to find joy along the path.

ACKNOWLEDGMENTS

This book began as a quiet act of healing.

After spending a decade in a life that no longer fit, my father's simple question – *"But are you happy?"* – cracked something open in me. It reminded me that I had the power to change, choose, let go, and begin again. And it's what planted the first seed of this book.

As I began building a new chapter of my life and business, I realized that so much of what had carried me through every reinvention – every challenge, every leap - was rooted in how I was raised and in the quiet lessons passed down from my Aita and my Ama.

To my father, Tiburcio Sarratea: your life, your spirit, your quiet leadership, and the way you simply *lived* what mattered – this book carries all of it. Because of you, I understood what it means to build something with heart. You are on every page.

To my mother – thank you for your steadiness, strength, and love.

To my sister, who has walked beside me my entire life, thank you for always showing up with honesty and care; you are my best friend.

To my husband, your belief in me has never wavered. Your support gave me room to write, dream, and keep walking this path.

To my amazing kids – You are my greatest teachers, my grounding force, and the joy I never knew I needed.

To the mentors, family, and friends who stood beside me: thank you. And to the early readers who saw the heart of this book and helped me bring it to life, thank you for your honest feedback, encouragement, and time. You helped me refine what mattered most.

And finally, to you, my readers, holding this book in your hands: thank you. Thank you for picking it up, reading it, and trusting me with a small part of your journey. I hope this book reminds you of your own quiet strength.

ABOUT THE AUTHOR

Anamarie Lopategui is a first-generation Basque American and the daughter of a Basque immigrant sheepherder whose quiet strength and integrity shaped her life. Drawing from a career that spans building and selling businesses, teaching in the classroom, and guiding others through life-changing decisions, she weaves together resilience, curiosity, and a deep respect for living in alignment with what matters most. Her experiences have taught her that success is not just measured in numbers, but in the everyday choices that shape our lives. *Built From the Quiet* is her first book.